Presented to:

By:

Date:

Letting Go & Trusting God

A DEVOTIONAL JOURNAL *for* LIFE'S TOUGH DECISIONS

Pamela L. McQuade

BARBOUR BOOKS
An Imprint of Barbour Publishing, Inc.

Introduction

*E*very day, we women make decisions that affect our lives, the lives of families and friends, the companies we work for, and the world. We are powerful people, even if we're sometimes unappreciated. We do everything from rocking the cradle to ruling the world.

I cannot know what decisions you face, nor, at this distance, can I advise you on how to solve thorny issues in your life. But I can share scriptures that help with making choices and offer some inspiration to encourage you along your decision-making way. I can tell you about the Lord who can do all the things I can't do in your life.

How do we make choices that honor God and enrich our lives? We turn to the Lord who controls our world and days, even the parts of them we have yet to experience. For He has the advice and wisdom we lack, and He knows every day of and bump in our lives.

Finally, with the inspiration here, I hope you'll be able to share God's truth "[that His] word is a lamp for my feet, a light on my path" (Psalm 119:105 NIV) and help others discover the best decision-making plan out there: Talking to the Lord on a day-by-day or even moment-by-moment basis.

Bundles of Decisions

God's Spirit doesn't make cowards out of us.
The Spirit gives us power, love, and self-control.
2 TIMOTHY 1:7 CEV

Here is the stuff we need for decision-making: courage, power, love, and self-control. Making good choices isn't for the faint of heart.

Decision-making often requires us to make many choices at a time, and that takes courage. That kind of decision overload can come when we get married, move, take care of an ailing family member, or lose a loved one. Lots of choices to make all at once; it's hard to know where to start, even when they're happy choices.

Simultaneously we may face relationship decisions with their own set of challenges. Sometimes they fall on top of other choices, making each more difficult. But God asks us to deal with all people and situations with love, no matter how burdened we feel or how hard the challenges seem. And instead of rushing into decisions or responding with unbridled emotions, He calls on us to use self-control.

Decision-making is often a balancing act in which we weigh one part of our lives against another, while constantly keeping the whole in mind. Only the Spirit's power, love, and self-control can provide us with all the necessary decision-making tools.

Though God gives us courage and strength for every choice He puts in our paths, it's up to us to seek His power, love, and self-control.

They're just waiting for us, in His hand.

Never Failures

For this God is our God for ever and ever;
he will be our guide even to the end.

PSALM 48:14 NIV

Some choices are ephemeral, only affecting a day, a week, or maybe even just a few minutes of our lives. But important choices have lasting impact: Where will we live? What kind of job will we have? Whom will we marry? Or will we stay single instead?

Sometimes those choices seem to easily make themselves for us: We leave school and a job just seems to turn up. But we still decide to take what's offered. When we walk into something easily, it could be a plan God has had for us all along or just a temporary stopping place. In time we may choose to move on, or we may be tempted to remain where life is comfortable. Decisions may not last forever, or they may be serious choices, the start of a lifetime of good things.

But whether things come to us easily or we struggle, we can be certain of one thing: God will be our lifelong guide.

When we come to a crossroads, we don't need to make a quick choice based only on our own experience. God offers us His immense store of knowledge and understanding. All we have to do is ask our Guide. Tapping into Him, we need not worry that one small choice will damage our lives unnecessarily: decisions made with God's wisdom are never failures.

Yes or No?

"But I say to you, do not swear at all: neither by heaven, for it is God's throne. . . . But let your 'Yes' be 'Yes,' and your 'No,' 'No.' For whatever is more than these is from the evil one."
MATTHEW 5:34, 37 NKJV

Often we don't take our promises very seriously. We tell a friend or coworker we'll help, but if life gets in the way, it's no big deal if we shrug off our commitment. We rearrange things to suit our needs, apologize, and never think twice of it. Promises don't mean that much, and we figure people will understand.

It wasn't that way in Jesus' day. The Jews back then knew that God had said they should keep any vows made in His name (Deuteronomy 23:23). To show they were serious, when they made a vow, they'd swear by various things of spiritual significance, like heaven or Jerusalem, but they'd leave His name out and think their unkept oaths avoided heavenly disapproval. Despite these verbal games, their track record was no better than ours.

Whether you call it a promise or a vow, God takes backing out seriously, as Jesus made clear in the Sermon on the Mount. "You don't have to swear, just say yes or no, but abide by your decision" is a simplified version of His message that left no one with a loophole.

As Christians, the way we act reflects on God; therefore, our every word should be our bond. So let's make decisions to help—or not to help—as life demands. But once we've made a choice, we need to follow through, in Jesus' name.

Separation

Then one of the twelve, called Judas Iscariot, went unto the chief priests, and said unto them, What will ye give me, and I will deliver him unto you? And they covenanted with him for thirty pieces of silver. And from that time he sought opportunity to betray him.
MATTHEW 26:14–16 KJV

*J*udas didn't just fall into betrayal or make a sudden mistake. Giving up his Master took planning. The wayward disciple visited Jesus' enemies to set things up. Then Israel's chief priests "covenanted" with the disciple to sell his Lord cheaply.

The betrayal started in one man's heart and mind, spread to others, and worked its way out in all their actions.

That plot should never have gotten beyond a mere, hastily pushed aside thought. But people are not perfect. Jealousy and self-interest draw every human into sin, as these Jewish spiritual leaders discovered. Or doubt fuels believers' motivations when they wonder if God has failed them. Some dissatisfaction filled Judas's soul and led to his downfall.

It's easy for us to pick on Judas, who had been with Jesus and clearly should have known better; but before we pick up a stone to throw at the failed disciple, we'd best take a long look at ourselves. Every wrong that takes hold of our minds and gets acted out in our lives makes traitors of us too.

We too have walked with the Savior. Will our thoughts hold fast to Him or slip as Judas's did?

Life Changer

As Jesus was walking beside the Sea of Galilee, he saw two brothers, Simon called Peter and his brother Andrew. They were casting a net into the lake, for they were fishermen. "Come, follow me," Jesus said, "and I will send you out to fish for people."

MATTHEW 4:18–19 NIV

Simon and Andrew heard Jesus' call unexpectedly. One day they were fishermen, toiling long hours in a boat, pulling in nets, and then hauling their catch to the marketplace to sell it. Their lives were predictable, and they seemed to have a secure future. The next day, they left all they knew and headed out to follow Jesus.

Many Christians today have a similar experience. One day they have little or no thought for God, the next they have committed their whole lives to Him. Coming to Jesus, whether it's a slow decision or an overnight one, means a huge change that influences an entire life. But all of us have to make a decision about Jesus: Will we accept Him, ignore Him, or intentionally deny Him? Even not making a decision is a decision, one that influences not only our lives but our eternal destiny.

Have you made that choice? Do you know that Jesus is your Savior, the One with whom you've thrown in your lot, just as His first disciples did? Or are you doubting or ignoring the One who calls you to drop your entangled nets and follow only Him?

Rich Love or Rich Lands

So Abram said to Lot, "Let's not have any quarreling between you and me, or between your herders and mine, for we are close relatives. Is not the whole land before you? Let's part company. If you go to the left, I'll go to the right; if you go to the right, I'll go to the left."
GENESIS 13:8–9 NIV

When he spoke these words, peaceable Abram had a lot to lose. And as a result of this speech, he temporarily lost some of the richest territory God had promised him. Lot took his uncle up on his generous offer and chose what looked like the very best property.

But, as Abram realized, sometimes even the richest things the world has to offer are not worth it, if it means destroying relationships or constantly having to fight with someone you love. He graciously let Lot have the best.

So Lot became a city dweller, while Abram remained in tents. But Lot's cushy land came with a terrible price. Eventually Abram's nephew discovered the danger that came with living in the well-watered plain of the Jordan, when he and his family had to flee the wickedness of its inhabitants. But his neighbors' sin had already permeated his family and all but destroyed it.

The greatest blessing was not the land but the relationship with God. While Abram got the lesser land, his faithfulness to the Lord remained unimpaired.

Do we want rich love or rich lands? And what are we willing to give for each?

Successful Plans

Plans go wrong for lack of advice; many advisers bring success.
PROVERBS 15:22 NLT

Ours is a "we can do it" society. Nothing seems beyond our ability, and we're encouraged to have a positive attitude about our skills and abilities—perhaps even when we're better gifted in another area.

Though there's nothing wrong with taking charge of our lives, we also need to know what we're doing. Since none of us can know everything about each decision we'll be faced with in life, it's not wise to assume that we can automatically do it all. That's why God tells us to look for wise advisers to steer us in the right direction.

The first adviser we need is God. He knows the directions our lives will take. For example, where will we live in twenty years? No human can know. But by following God and seeking His wisdom, we can live today in a way that prepares us for the future. Choices that follow His will never fail.

But we also need the humility to ask the help of people who really know about any choices we need to make today. Maybe we need to consult several people to come to a good decision about the home we need today. Then we can weigh advice, pray about the best direction, and come to the wisest choice.

No human knows as much as God, but people can still help turn us in the right direction. Let's look for those God sends our way to give us success.

Hard Work or Poverty?

Good planning and hard work lead to prosperity,
but hasty shortcuts lead to poverty.
PROVERBS 21:5 NLT

*I*t's been a terribly hectic week, but this project is almost out the door. Just a few minor details to wrap up, and the weekend is all mine, Jason thinks. *I certainly deserve a break after all the long hours I've put in.*

Just then, his boss stops by to remind him of one more detail. "It shouldn't take more than an hour," he encourages his worker. "After all you've done, it will just be the icing on the cake that might win us this bid."

Icing on the cake, all right, Jason thinks. *That's about what it is— icing on an awful week. Why do I do this job anyway? There's got to be some shortcut that will get me out the door in just a few minutes,* he grumbles to himself.

Does Jason hear temptation calling? Or is he simply so caught up in his own desires that he doesn't understand that one more hour of hard work could bring success to his company—and himself—while shortchanging the job could destroy it all?

Usually we need to do the hard work this verse talks about at the least convenient moment. Hard moments never come when life is easy. But choosing to hang on in a tough time may be blessed by God because we made the right choice in a difficult moment.

Yes, shortcuts provide easy ways out. But let's make sure they don't result in our giving less than our best. After all, we are His handiwork.

Willing to Risk?

*Give my greetings to Priscilla and Aquila, my co-workers in the
ministry of Christ Jesus. In fact, they once risked their lives for me.
I am thankful to them, and so are all the Gentile churches.*
ROMANS 16:3–4 NLT

After Aquila and his wife, Priscilla, had fled from Rome following
Claudius Caesar's deportation of the Jews, this tent-making
couple met Paul. We don't know if they received Christ through
the apostle's ministry, but clearly they were drawn to his message
and became strong Christians and active church members who
were skilled in doctrine (Acts 18:24–26). Paul valued them as close
friends and coworkers, and the couple established a congregation of
believers in their home.

At some point, though we don't know what they did, Priscilla
and Aquila made a choice that put their own lives at risk. Their
bravery must have been well-known to the Gentile churches, who
appreciated the couple's steadfastness to their leader and friend.

When Priscilla and Aquila faced a difficult, faith-challenging
decision, they made a faith-based choice. However large the risk,
it proved right and worth it, as God protected them and brought
blessing to the church.

We may not have to risk our lives, but, like Priscilla and Aquila,
will we make decisions that are based on our faith and that testify
to it? Sometimes God asks us to make hard choices that risk things
that seem almost as important as life to us.

Will we risk something for Jesus? Or is life as it is simply too
comfortable?

Choosing Praise

James son of Zebedee and his brother John (to them he gave the name Boanerges, which means "sons of thunder").
MARK 3:17 NIV

What did Jesus, who rarely criticized His disciples, mean by calling these brothers "sons of thunder"? Many people believe John and his brother Andrew had a tough time holding on to their tempers.

How many of us know the dangers of quick but ill-thought-out speech? Words spill out of our mouths before we can slap our hands over them. Or we leap into speech before our minds are fully engaged and end up looking foolish.

But God, who gives us "a sound mind" (2 Timothy 1:7 NKJV) and helps us put a guard on our mouths (Psalm 141:3), can give us the self-control we need. The problem isn't God's willingness to help but our unwillingness to give up the "joys" of wrong speech. Part of us likes to open our mouths and give honest opinions to an aggravating person. Or we'll let off steam on a subject we should have thought out more carefully. But afterward, instead of feeling brave and honest, our decision to speak out boldly makes us feel embarrassed and unclean.

We can cooperate with God's plan for our words or rebel against it. Rebellion brings lots of thunder and very few blessings. Well-thought-out speech that comes from a heart aligned with God's will brings much more fruitful results.

Our mouths were made for praise, not condemnation or foolishness. Which will we choose?

Nothing to Fear

*"The L*ORD* himself goes before you and will be with
you; he will never leave you nor forsake you.
Do not be afraid; do not be discouraged."*
DEUTERONOMY 31:8 NIV

ou really didn't have much to say about your decision. Life
just cornered you, and you went the only way you could,
boxed in by circumstance. Now, fear fills your heart when you look
at your situation.

The Israelites whom Moses spoke these words to knew just how
that felt. Their parents and grandparents spent forty years circling
in a desert because of one grave, disobedient act. As this group faced
crossing into the Promised Land, anything might have seemed better
than wandering for forty more years, yet they must have had serious
doubts. After all, wasn't this dangerous, to invade a land filled with
pagan people?

Making that river crossing that would lead them into a land filled
with enemies was a terrifying prospect. Then their leader, Moses,
told them he wasn't going to be with them.

There was a lot to be discouraged about! But Moses told them
their only hope was in the One who had brought them to this point.
Maybe they felt nervous about trusting in the Lord, who had kept
them walking in circles for so long. Doubt may have filled their hearts.
But Moses promised that God would go before them and never leave
them. There was nothing to fear.

That promise works in our lives too, when we feel doubtful and
cornered. God has never deserted us, and He never will. How we feel
about our situation is less important than His faithfulness.

Emoticons?

〜〜〜〜〜〜〜〜〜〜

*Therefore, as God's chosen people, holy and dearly
loved, clothe yourselves with compassion, kindness,
humility, gentleness and patience.*

COLOSSIANS 3:12 NIV

❧

Feeling angry or bitter? Maybe you'd like to slap a false emoticon on your face and pretend you're the ultimate happy Christian.

But that cheesy little computer smiley face wouldn't solve the problem. Inside, you'd still feel mad or bitter. Even if you gritted your teeth and said the "right" thing, others would know you were being a hypocrite as you struggled to show compassion to the person who just took advantage of you or faced off with a coworker who got the job wrong for the third time in a row.

God's clothing isn't a cover-up but a sign of His cleansing. He never calls us to feel an emotion He won't empower us to have.

Through this verse, our Lord calls us to choose positive emotions and make them part of our daily existence. That doesn't mean we must grit our teeth and spit out the right words, even though they aren't in our hearts. Such legalism only makes us frustrated.

Putting on the clothes of a godly life takes time and means we have to deal with sin. We won't be completely garbed in lovely robes of humility, gentleness, and patience seconds after our conversion, but as we make godly actions our goal and love the Lord who commanded us to have them, they'll slowly become part of our everyday lives. Then we won't need any emoticons; our emotions will be true and grounded in the One who gave them to us.

What emotions are you choosing today?

Peaceful Feast

Oh, those holidays when family members descend on your home. Many are folks you love to share it with. But just one difficult person can make your feast more like a trial than a celebration.

Faced with such a situation, it's time to remember this verse and decide to have a meal filled with love. Maybe you can't stop that distant relative's critical mouth or change her mind. But you can choose to respond with reason and love instead of helping the emotional fires burn. Perhaps you can take control before everyone in the room is filled with ire.

You might help things by placing that tart-tongued person at the table next to a family member who's known for having a long stream of patience (and put someone fun on his other side). Maybe, on your challenging person's other side, you need to connect her up with the one person in the family who really seems to like her. If you have another wise Christian in the family who understands the situation, perhaps you can work together to see that emotions don't run so high that they ruin the day for anyone.

Hospitality isn't always easy, but it can be an opportunity to show a lonely, harsh person love. Perhaps God wants to use this event to show your guest the joy of His love.

When you see a change in that difficult person's life, what a delight it will be to know it came from the simple love shown at a feast you let her share.

Wisdom in Silence

Even fools are thought wise if they keep silent,
and discerning if they hold their tongues.
PROVERBS 17:28 NIV

We think of decision-makers as bold people who speak out often and clearly, using powerful words. But God gives us another view: good decision-makers also need to know when to bite their tongues and avoid comments.

That may be the hardest decision of all, since we all like to air our opinions, even the less-than-perfect ones. Passionate people have passionate opinions, whether they are right or wrong. We all can stick to an imperfect idea, and sometimes opposition simply makes us hold on harder.

Though passion can communicate effectively, sometimes we need to recognize that we might need more knowledge than passion and should keep our mouths shut. Even a foolish person who has no idea what's going on may look temporarily wise by simply shutting her mouth.

That doesn't mean we shouldn't make decisions or that we should remain permanently silent, but we need to understand our own limitations and know when we need time to research the truth and learn more about a situation. Perhaps we simply need to bring an idea to God in prayer or search His Word to find His way.

Silence isn't a permanent solution. Eventually we'll need to open our mouths and remove all doubt, one way or the other. But sometimes being quiet allows God to work in wiser, gentler ways that get the job done much more effectively.

Let's tap into that powerful wisdom.

Prayer Choices

"Solomon, ask for anything you want,
and I will give it to you."
1 KINGS 3:5 CEV

*G*od gave Solomon this opportunity to write a blank check for himself. And Solomon made a good request, one God approved of and that put the king in the spotlight.

But what if the king had asked to remain faithful to God, instead of asking for wisdom? Had he been able to look down the years and see the future, the wise king might have changed his request. Lack of faithfulness to God became wise Solomon's fatal flaw.

Notice that unlike the fairy tale's genie in the bottle, God did not limit how many gifts Solomon could ask for. Could he have asked for faithfulness, so that he could have God's wisdom to rule the land wisely? He might not have been known as the wisest man in the world; instead, Solomon might have gotten a reputation for devotion to his Lord. Though that might have meant having a less flashy reputation, the king's example might have forestalled the paganism that influenced his own life and all but destroyed his country in the years following his death.

Let's learn from Solomon's example. God tells us to ask for all our needs. Do we do that? Are we fearful to ask for too much, or do we recognize our need for our heavenly Father's mercy and bring all our cares to Him? If we ask only for those things that are in God's will, we cannot be greedy. Seeking to obey and serve Him is just what He desires in our lives.

Sacrifice of Praise

*Through Jesus, therefore, let us continually offer to God
a sacrifice of praise—the fruit of lips that openly profess
his name. And do not forget to do good and to share
with others, for with such sacrifices God is pleased.*
HEBREWS 13:15–16 NIV

Life is difficult—work is challenging, friends are demanding, extra expenses are falling on our checkbooks at the worst time. Is it time for us to start complaining, returning the pressure, or shutting out the world, refusing to help others?

Maybe we need a break for a short time—an evening alone with a good book or a morning to sleep in. Perhaps some extra private prayer time would give a new perspective, or maybe we need to ask a friend or family member to share in a special time of prayer. One thing's certain: choosing to react with anger and irritation won't put troubles to rights.

As we bring our needs before God, let's not forget how many other troubles He has brought us through. Let's look back on the past and take courage, thanking God that just as He's helped us with stress and troubles before, He will do so again.

As His children, we know He will never leave or forsake us, though the way may seem long. Like a mother who cannot forget her children, God cannot forget us (Isaiah 49:15).

When we cling to Him like babes whose sustenance depends on Him alone, He will fill our hearts and spirits again.

Character Development

Joseph found favor in his eyes and became his attendant.
Potiphar put him in charge of his household,
and he entrusted to his care everything he owned.
GENESIS 39:4 NIV

Joseph must have been an amazing decision-maker. His story shows so many places where, instead of responding with anger or despair, he made powerful life choices.

Sold into slavery, this Israelite could have allowed fear of the future or frustration to take over his life. Instead, he decided to put his heart into working for another man, a pagan with a flirtatious wife.

Many less-than-perfect elements filled Joseph's life, but God had given him to honest Potiphar, who trusted the blessings Joseph brought into his life and who seemed to have understood Joseph's character, as well as his wife's. Having put his trust in the Israelite, he did not withdraw it easily—instead of taking Joseph's life, he spared the slave his wife wrongfully accused.

Had Joseph shared his past with his master? Scripture doesn't tell us. But Potiphar saw the wise choices made by his slave and understood that attacking his wife did not fit with all he knew of the man who efficiently ran the household. Joseph's choices spoke loudly of his character.

Our decision-making also speaks of our own character development. Will our testimony show others the faithfulness of our God or our own lack of character strength? Even if we fail, when we cling to God, as Joseph did, the end of our story will be strong.

Trust but Verify

~~~~~~~~~~~~~~~~~

Now Joseph gave these instructions to the steward of his house:
"Fill the men's sacks with as much food as they can carry,
and put each man's silver in the mouth of his sack.
Then put my cup, the silver one, in the mouth of the youngest
one's sack, along with the silver for his grain."

GENESIS 44:1–2 NIV

As Joseph gave this command, his heart may have been in his mouth. Would his half brothers prove they had learned from their mistake in sending him into slavery, or were they the same unreliable men he'd dealt with years before? The cup left in Benjamin's bag was designed to test the brothers' character, and perhaps save Benjamin from a similar fate if they proved unfaithful. When their youngest brother was accused of theft, would his half brothers stand beside him or silently watch him go into slavery?

Egypt's prime minister was no fool where his family was concerned. But he also understood God's forgiveness and the need to pass it on to his siblings. So he created this perfect plan that helped him assess the situation. Joseph wanted to trust but also had to verify their characters.

Just because we love God and follow His commands, we are not expected to accept just any promise from people who have failed us. That's not faith or forgiveness but foolishness. Trust is earned, not given on a whim.

People are complex beings who often fail us and themselves. Only God's wisdom sees into others' hearts. Before making a major decision involving others, let's verify it with Him.

Perfect Solution

"You intended to harm me, but God intended it for good to accomplish what is now being done, the saving of many lives. So then, don't be afraid. I will provide for you and your children." And [Joseph] reassured them and spoke kindly to them.

GENESIS 50:20–21 NIV

If we had been sold into slavery, how many of us would have this attitude toward the people who sold us? Joseph's attitude is amazing. Was he some kind of superhero?

Joseph had probably pondered his brothers' actions for many years. As he worked for Potiphar, sat in jail, and finally became Egypt's second-in-command, he could never forget how he had unwillingly come to Egypt. But instead of falling into bitterness, Joseph embraced the opportunities before him. God blessed him for his attitude, and Joseph prospered.

Maybe success took the edge off the pain of his brothers' betrayal. Perhaps he saw that his own pride had contributed to the situation. Somehow, God helped Joseph come to terms with his less-than-happy family life.

Finally, Joseph's brothers understood how wrong they had been, and the family was reunited. But when their father died, they still feared retribution. Did they know Joseph so little? Or were they thinking of what their own reactions would have been, had they been treated so badly?

Joseph came to terms with the painful part of his past, and so should we. But that's only possible if we give all our hurts to our Lord and seek His perfect solution. Only He can help us forgive hurts that are too painful for us to share.

Brave but Gentle

"If it pleases the king," replied Esther, "let the king, together with Haman, come today to a banquet I have prepared for him."

ESTHER 5:4 NIV

When her cousin Mordecai called on Esther to approach the king and save her people, the queen's heart filled with fear. But stirring up bravery in her heart, she committed herself to act, though she risked losing her life.

However, the wise queen approached her touchy husband slowly and carefully, asking him and the Jews' enemy, Haman, to a banquet. Twice, she wined and dined the men before she brought up the real issue.

We may wonder how the Jewish queen could host the man who wanted to wipe her people off the face of the earth. Those had to have been the tensest days in Esther's life, but she knew the work of those two nights could save many lives. To convince the king to stop his favorite from killing her people, she knew she'd have to build his trust in her first. He needed a gentle touch.

When we face confrontations, especially nasty ones, sometimes it's good to take the issue slowly instead of barging in and making a bad situation worse. Diplomatic measures may bring others to our side and express kindness rather than impatient demands.

In another time and place, many people both within and outside his circle made violent efforts to stop Hitler from continuing the conflict and persecution that took the lives of so many Jews. None worked.

What if there had been a brave but gentle Esther to turn his heart from evil?

Where We Go from Here

During the night, Paul had a vision of someone from
Macedonia who was standing there and begging him,
"Come over to Macedonia and help us!"
ACTS 16:9 CEV

Where should we go from here? Paul and his companions had been asking themselves. Though they needed another place to minister, the Spirit had blocked them from Phrygia, Galatia, and Bithynia. The faithful group of missionaries must have wondered what was going on. Weren't they trying to build God's kingdom? Why were their plans always flopping?

God finally sent Paul a vision, calling the men to a place they probably hadn't much thought of. While they looked to minister in Asia Minor, God was calling them to northern Greece. The small band crossed the Aegean to Samothrace and then Philippi, preaching there and making their first European convert.

Sometimes, as with Paul and his companions, our own plans are less challenging than the ones God has in mind for us. We're sticking to our comfort zone while He wants us out there in a new place. Maybe that's why our plans haven't evolved so smoothly. Or maybe, if we've had challenges up to our chins, God is simply slowing things down for a while. He knows we need a rest before moving on. Or perhaps He's just building our strength in another kind of challenge. God always knows where we are going, even when we don't.

Whatever our plans may be, God always has the best one for us. Could we simply need to wait a bit for the answer to our prayers?

Bearing Witness

Mary Magdalene came and told the disciples that she had seen the Lord, and that He had spoken these things to her.
JOHN 20:18 NKJV

A faithful message bearer, Mary ran to the apostles with wonderful news: Jesus was risen from the dead! But instead of joining her in joy, her friends doubted (Mark 16:11). Mary's good news must have fallen like a thump to the bottom of her heart.

That moment of testimony and rejection is the last we know of Mary. Perhaps she went on to be a faithful member of the first-century church, sharing the good news God showed her that morning. Scripture doesn't say.

We've never had the awe-inspiring task of sharing the news of Jesus' resurrection with those closest to Him. But we've shared that most important message with others and been faced with doubt. We've told family members and friends of our conversion and had them look at us in horror. Or we've had to face down unbelievers at school or in the workplace. Bearing witness isn't always received with kudos.

When others don't take our message seriously or don't appreciate the message and take it out on the messenger, we can curl up in a ball and hide our faith or continue to live it out day by day, knowing that every conversion is in God's hands, not our own. Sometimes a consistent, loving relationship works where preaching never will.

Others' reactions are not under our control, but ours are. Will we choose to remain steady, faithful witnesses who can draw others to Him?

Useful to God

Apollos started speaking bravely in the Jewish meeting place. But when Priscilla and Aquila heard him, they took him to their home and helped him understand God's Way even better.

ACTS 18:26 CEV

Skilled speaker Apollos came to Ephesus, preaching the scriptures. His doctrine was solid but incomplete: he knew of John's baptism but not the coming of the Holy Spirit. So teachers Priscilla and Aquila brought him into their home and helped him understand the entire Christian message.

Instead of being offended, Apollos drank in the Good News and applied himself to learning it. As he grew in Christ, he became a valuable preacher. Some Corinthians even claimed to follow him when division began in that church (1 Corinthians 3). But instead of setting himself up in opposition to Paul, Apollos continued to humbly serve everyone and help the apostle. Paul, recognizing his spiritual strength, freely encouraged Apollos to visit the church in Corinth (1 Corinthians 16:12).

Choosing not to become spiritually proud and putting someone else's skills and blessings first is a decision that shows our spiritual tenor. We'd all like to see our spiritual gifts valued and appreciated, and that can bring us into conflict with other gifted people. Satan often successfully uses pride to divide the Church.

Putting ourselves ahead of others cannot grow the Church or bring doubters to Christ. Only when God gives and blesses the gifts and our authority can He use us to touch many lives.

We all have a ministry that's useful to our Lord. Let's determine to let God use us as He sees fit.

Lost Desire

David. . .gave Solomon the plans for building the main rooms of the temple, including the porch, the storerooms, the rooms upstairs and downstairs, as well as the most holy place. He gave Solomon his plans for the courtyards and the open areas around the temple, and for the rooms to store the temple treasures and gifts that had been dedicated to God.

1 Chronicles 28:11–12 cev

Building God's temple was the desire of David's heart. He felt it wasn't right to build himself a fine palace and leave God with no formal place of worship. So David developed detailed plans for the temple.

What a disappointment it must have been when God told David he couldn't start work on the building that meant the most to him. But David never consigned the plans to the fire or resented the news that his son Solomon would take on the task. Instead, David graciously conferred the plans to his son, along with the kingdom. When Solomon was ready to build, he'd have all the blueprints to hand to the builders. David must have realized that creating such a building would only bring luster to Solomon's name. The aged king set him up for success.

Like David, we too probably won't get to do everything we want in life. Sometimes we have to leave a church ministry and pass it on to another, or we are displaced from a job. Will we react graciously or grievously? What will our legacy be to those who follow us?

Grabbing Choices

*The woman stared at the fruit. It looked beautiful and tasty.
She wanted the wisdom that it would give her, and she ate
some of the fruit. Her husband was there with her,
so she gave some to him, and he ate it too.*

GENESIS 3:6 CEV

If anyone made a truly bad decision, it was Eve. Offered the fruit of the tree of knowledge of good and evil, she found it appealing. Without a second thought, ignoring God's warning, she grabbed this tasty fruit. Both she and Adam joined in sin as they bit into the flavorful produce. A single moment impacted not only their own lives but the lives of every person since.

Every day of our lives we make choices. Some look so good, so tempting. Others seem so ordinary, there seems to be no question about what we should do. But in most choices there's an opportunity to sin, even unintentionally.

As with Eve, our choices are important because they can change the direction of our lives and those of our families, friends, and coworkers. They can even change the lives of people we've never met.

You've heard the expression "you can't judge a book by its cover." Neither can you make a great choice by falling for its initial shiny appeal. Things that look good on the outside may turn sour once we bite into them a bit more deeply.

Instead of grabbing at the first rosy option, we need to consider the wisdom God has already given us and the guidance He offers today. Then we'll make the best choice for us and those we love.

Shut Your Mouth?

*Miriam and Aaron began to talk against Moses because of his
Cushite wife, for he had married a Cushite. "Has the LORD
spoken only through Moses?" they asked. "Hasn't he also
spoken through us?" And the LORD heard this. . . .
The anger of the LORD burned against them.*
NUMBERS 12:1–2, 9 NIV

Complaints, complaints, complaints. We hear them everywhere,
even in church; complaints about the pastor, the leadership,
and other believers in the communion can bring bitterness to God's
people.

None of this is new. Even humble Moses, who led a whole nation
toward the Promised Land, had critics in his closest relatives, who
didn't like his choice of bride. But there was more than that to their
criticism of their brother: They *really* didn't like the fact that God had
given him authority over themselves. *They* wanted to be in charge.

Before his brother and sister's complaints got passed around the
camp or were brought to the prophet, God stepped in, calling a
meeting between the three siblings and Himself. God stood up for
His prophet, and Miriam walked out of that meeting covered with
leprosy.

Make no doubt about it, when we criticize others, we do so
because we've made a choice to open our mouths and spew out
harsh words. It's not a decision God approves of, as He graphically
illustrated on Miriam's flesh.

Before we open our lips in complaint, maybe we should remember
Miriam and consider shutting our mouths and confessing our sins
instead.

A Balanced Life

*"But seek first his kingdom and his righteousness,
and all these things will be given to you as well."*

MATTHEW 6:33 NIV

Our minds easily fill up with plans to gain all the things we need: food, clothes, transportation, money to pay bills—the list is a long one. If we're not careful, we may begin focusing on things, to the exclusion of our spiritual lives and relationships. When what we own becomes more important than God's priorities, we easily land in trouble.

Getting things may be important to us, but giving them is important to God. As large as our needs loom in our eyes, God knows every one of them. And compared to His ability to fill every requirement for our lives, our needs are incredibly tiny. What could we need that God could not bring into our lives in the proper time? And if we don't get something, is that "need" just an unnecessary extra?

When we choose to seek God's kingdom and righteousness first, all our needs eventually fall into line. We may not dine in elegant restaurants, but we will have food to eat. We may never own a summer home, a yacht, and other unnecessary extras, but our hearts may be full.

Benefiting God's kingdom is more important than selfishly worrying over the things we don't have. Once we put God first in our lives, we'll be amazed at how balanced our days become.

Wonderful Things

*Lord, you are my God; I will exalt you and praise
your name, for in perfect faithfulness you have
done wonderful things, things planned long ago.*
Isaiah 25:1 niv

Life seems out of control, our lives spiraling into a colorless, cold place. Doubt fills our minds. Was this where God wanted us to be? Did we wander off in the wrong direction, though we thought we chose to obey God?

Isaiah knew all about living in that out-of-control place. Israel had become disobedient and rebellious, constantly at odds with her Maker, and the Israelites objected long and loudly. As the prophet quickly discovered, ministering to these miserable people was no picnic.

Putting up with such folks might easily have caused Isaiah to lose his moral and spiritual compass. Doubtless, dealing with them sometimes made him feel as if he was whirling in circles too. He prophesied the earth's terrible destruction in chapter 24.

But when the prophet felt the spinning start, he knew where to look. Instead of putting his trust in the world around him or any person, Isaiah looked to the Lord. In the next chapter, the prophet followed his dire predictions with a song of hope that promised God would not forget His people.

Just as God did not overlook his prophet or the people Isaiah served, He does not forget us either. His faithful plans order our lives too, even if our lives seem to spin in circles. No matter how many dark clouds appear on the horizon, our faithful God still does wonderful things.

A Better Future

Five-year plans, future projections, when we'd like to marry, have children—or even when we'd like to see our children have children—or plans to have no child at all: no matter whether we write them down or just keep them in our heads and hearts, we all have plans and desires we want to see fulfilled in our lives. The decisions we make are often motivated by our personal goals, and we do the best we can to further those ends.

But sometimes, no matter how good and clear our planning is, those plans persistently don't happen. Maybe Mr. Right doesn't come along, or the job we end up in isn't the one we thought we should have. Or our plans seem just about to work out, but everything falls through.

We can beat ourselves up over this "failure," lamenting our view of the way things should be, or we can accept that God's plan and ours were different. Maybe He's got something else in mind for our lives that we need to discover.

Fighting against God's plan gets us nowhere. But following this plan we never thought of brings us to a prosperous end—the one He designed—filled with hope and a better future than we could have imagined.

Wrong Choice?

And the people of Berea were more open-minded than those in Thessalonica, and they listened eagerly to Paul's message. They searched the Scriptures day after day to see if Paul and Silas were teaching the truth.

ACTS 17:11 NLT

The Bereans had a decision to make: Would they believe Paul and follow his teachings or decide he was well-meaning but wrong? Knowing their spiritual lives would be profoundly affected by their choice, they looked into the matter. These eager, careful students seemed concerned about getting things right.

Not long afterward, the angry Jewish leaders of Thessalonica, the city from which Paul and his companions had been forced to run, heard Paul had moved on to Berea. They followed him and began turning crowds against the apostle, until Paul had to move on again. Silas and Timothy completed the mission in Berea.

The scriptures tell us nothing more about careful Berea. Did a few people come to Christ, or did everyone reject Him? We will only know in eternity.

But we can take this truth from Berea: our spiritual choices are important, and we should make well-informed decisions. If attacks come upon our faith, we need to stand firm.

Any Bereans who allowed mere humans to distract them from the message Paul brought were the great losers. They proved they weren't as open-minded to the Gospel as it initially seemed if their eager attention was captured by Jewish legalism.

Making an eternally wrong choice was not the decision the Bereans intended, and it's one we shouldn't aim for either.

Wholehearted Sacrifice?

I beseech you therefore, brethren, by the mercies of God,
that ye present your bodies a living sacrifice, holy,
acceptable unto God, which is your reasonable service.
ROMANS 12:1 KJV

*G*iving our whole bodies to God? That's a serious sacrifice that hits us right where we live.

But God tells us it's more than that. The apostle Paul wrote: "Do you not know that your bodies are temples of the Holy Spirit, who is in you, whom you have received from God? You are not your own; you were bought at a price. Therefore honor God with your bodies" (1 Corinthians 6:19–20 NIV). How can we escape God if He's right here, inside us?

There's an inexplicable link between the body and spirit. Neither in body nor spirit can we "escape" God. David knew that (Psalm 139:7–13). So giving Him a gift of our whole bodies, which are already His temples, is merely the natural outcome of our relationship with Him.

That's not to say that taking that step is easy. Often our bodies want to drag us in another direction, and our minds head in a not-so-holy way, leading our spirits astray with them. Tiredness makes us cranky and less than kind with our mouths. Our sexual desires can wreak havoc, though our spirits long to obey.

Choosing to worship God with our whole beings may be impossible in our own power, but the Spirit's strength enables us to do the very thing we fear and fail at so often. In Him comes success beyond anything we could imagine through our own abilities.

Taste and See

O taste and see that the LORD is good:
blessed is the man that trusteth in him.
PSALM 34:8 KJV

Decision-making comes in all shapes and sizes. Sometimes it's fun, when life is opening up before us and blue skies lie ahead. But when a family member is ill or financial woes loom large, the choices are harder and don't have much joy in them.

But whatever we face and whatever choice we make, every change that lies before us comes from the God who controls the universe. He puts the choices in our lives, and it's up to us to make them. We are wise to ask His help ahead of time so we can make right decisions that glorify Him.

Even when we make mistakes, God can help us recover. Even when we are not good, He is. The apostle Paul tells us: "In all things God works for the good of those who love him, who have been called according to his purpose" (Romans 8:28 NIV). He has chosen to love us, so He works for our good. We may encounter some detours on our journey, but there is nothing He cannot turn to good if we turn to Him for forgiveness and aid.

God may let us wander in our own direction, but He will always be standing at every dead end, calling us back to His best path. He is always good, and so will our way be, when we trust in Him.

Let's taste of His goodness today.

For Such a Time

*Now the king was attracted to Esther. . .and she won his
favor and approval more than any of the other virgins.
So he set a royal crown on her head and made her queen.*
ESTHER 2:17 NIV

Beautiful Esther won royal approval and became a queen. But
she had no say in what happened to her from the time she
was brought to the king's harem to the time she was married. And
the man she married was no "prince" when it came to dealing with
women. Look at how he'd mistreated his former wife, Vashti.

Trapped in marriage to a man who did not share her faith or
values, Esther probably didn't have an easy time. Though she lived
in a palace, she had to bear with the choices of a dictatorial king,
and her life was less than peaceful. Called upon to visit the king
and ask him to save her people, the queen quaked. Obviously the
tender days of newlywed romance had not lasted long, since she
feared Xerxes would kill her for appearing before him.

Though she'd had no say in the planning of this situation, God
had. Clearly, as her cousin foretold, He had put her in this position
"for such a time as this" (Esther 4:14 NIV).

Have little or no part in decision-making? Perhaps, like Esther,
it's time to accept the situation as one God has put in your life so
He can use you too. You may be where you are for just such a time.

Changing Truth

Then the woman took the two men and hid them. So she said,
"Yes, the men came to me, but I did not know where they
were from. And it happened as the gate was being shut,
when it was dark, that the men went out."
JOSHUA 2:4–5 NKJV

What does it take to make a woman become a traitor to her own people? That has to be a tough decision—one a smart woman wouldn't make lightly. Yet when soldiers came to Rahab's door, seeking the Jews who were hidden in her home, she didn't hesitate to misdirect them.

Rahab wasn't just risking her life for any strangers. This woman understood that the Jews had conquered kingdoms of their Promised Land because God had given it to them. Somehow God had reached out to this pagan woman and shown her the truth.

Rahab responded to the spies, "I know that the LORD has given you the land, that the terror of you has fallen on us, and that all the inhabitants of the land are fainthearted because of you" (v. 9 NKJV). Fear may have driven her to action, but acknowledging the truth changed her and put her where God wanted her to be.

Scripture isn't necessarily advocating treason, but, as Rahab found, God's truth confronts us and commands us. It comes first in our lives—not our country or anything else.

When we make our decisions with God's truth in mind, we'll make the best ones.

Serving Others

All the believers were united in heart and mind. And they felt that what they owned was not their own, so they shared everything they had. . . . There were no needy people among them, because those who owned land or houses would sell them and bring the money to the apostles to give to those in need.

ACTS 4:32, 34–35 NLT

*C*an you imagine freely sharing all you owned? The lives of these early Christians stand as a testimony to both generosity and need—and they challenge us when we think about how hard that kind of giving and taking would be to do.

Some, out of their great need, had to humbly accept the gifts of others. There was no welfare in those days, and in order to live, the poorest members of the new faith had to depend on their coreligionists. It may have been hard to accept charity, but the unity of heart and mind in the congregation must have helped ease that pain.

Those with land or homes, on the other hand, clung to nothing, but served the needy by sharing. In giving up their property, they also lost control of how it was used, yet they trusted those in command of church funds.

How could those who benefited fail to love those who gave? How could they fail to serve others who gave them all they needed to survive? The love in the church grew by such actions.

How can our churches grow from our generosity, whether we have money or service to offer?

Wink at Sin?

*But there was a certain man named Ananias who, with his wife,
Sapphira, sold some property. He brought part of the money
to the apostles, claiming it was the full amount.
With his wife's consent, he kept the rest.*

ACTS 5:1–2 NLT

Ananias and Sapphira's story begins quietly with the sale of their
property. Since others in the church were doing the same, it
was not an unusual event. But things change when the character
of the sellers becomes clear. This couple was a matched pair of liars
who exaggerated their sacrifice in order to gain the glory of others'
good opinions.

Choosing generosity has a price. When you sell land and give
the proceeds to your church, you no longer have any land, money,
or even the right to say how the money is used. This couple couldn't
face losing that much, but neither did they want to look cheap, so
honesty became the first casualty of their moral weakness.

*It's a small sin, isn't it? After all, who will find out about it? And if
anyone does, the price will be small,* Ananias and Sapphira probably
thought. Maybe they even had a plan to get out of that situation.

But they had not counted on the Almighty's knowledge of their
deed. God made an example of them, and within minutes of speaking
their lies, they were both dead.

Do we wink at our own sins, perhaps counting the cost and
figuring it's worth it? Even if we don't lose our physical lives, what
spiritual death do we experience?

A Sure Proof

*Faith makes us sure of what we hope for and
gives us proof of what we cannot see.*

HEBREWS 11:1 CEV

Wouldn't it be nice if we made decisions and saw wonderful results in just a short time? But decision-making doesn't work that way. Sometimes we see good results right away and negative results we hadn't expected down the road. Other times we don't see many results at all for many years.

Decision-making requires much faith—when we're making those choices and as we wait for the results (or when we have to fine-tune decisions because something wasn't quite right). We make our choices and live with them. But happily, few decisions can't be changed or otherwise dealt with. When all else fails, we have the option of confessing our wrongdoing and turning around through God's forgiveness.

God challenges us with decisions to make us "sure of what we hope for" and give us "proof of what we cannot see." As our daily lives take form around our choices, we begin to see how God works within us and proves the future He has laid before us in eternity.

As we look ahead and hope God's promises will be fulfilled despite our flawed decision-making process, God gives us sure proof that He will always be faithful, even when we fail. As we trust in Him when we make errors, we learn which of us is really trustworthy, and we put our faith in the One whom we cannot see.

Right and Good

"Do what is right and good in the sight of the LORD,
that it may be well with you, and that you
may go in and possess the good land."
DEUTERONOMY 6:18 NKJV

Sometimes doing right just doesn't seem worth it. That's the reason the proverb "no good deed will go unpunished" is so popular. Often we do the right thing, only to have it backfire on us. We lend a tool to a neighbor and never see it again. We help coworkers, only to have them take all the credit.

How, we ask ourselves, can these be good choices?

When we think in worldly terms, certainly they don't look good. We appear to be rubes who are taken advantage of as a result of our own stupidity. Worldly persons, we assume, quickly identify and avoid such situations.

But if we're Christians, we don't have the option to selfishly step back and avoid helping others. God calls us to step forward and help people, knowing that sometimes they'll take advantage of us (Matthew 5:41).

Though we may sometimes be taken advantage of, we need to keep on doing the right thing—that which God calls us to do. As we serve others, sometimes get taken advantage of, and forgive, we show forth God's compassion and love. And He promises that even if we do miss out on something as a result of our generosity, all will be well—after all, He gives us the land of eternity.

Right Choice?

*Judah said, "What will we gain if we kill our brother and hide
his body? Let's sell him to the Ishmaelites and not harm him.
After all, he is our brother." And the others agreed.*
GENESIS 37:26–27 CEV

Perhaps because they were faced with their brother Reuben's
objections to killing Joseph, the other brothers backed down
and decided to sell their half brother into slavery instead. A kinder,
gentler decision? Not by much. While his brothers roamed freely
with their flocks, Joseph would serve powerful men in a strange,
pagan land. Instead of going in and out freely, he'd move at someone
else's command and even spend time in jail, though he had done
no wrong. And all Joseph's suffering was simply so that his brothers
wouldn't have to live under his authority—a prophecy God brought
to pass in the end anyway. As hard as they tried to avoid God's will,
the rebellious brothers couldn't.

Sometimes our disobedience defers a problem or issue in our lives,
but that doesn't mean it disappears entirely. If God has ordained it
as part of a plan for our lives, it may return to us again, until God
shows us the truth we missed. That's what happened to Joseph's
brothers.

In sending Joseph into slavery, the brothers may have turned
away from making the worst choice possible, but they still didn't
make the right one. Through a famine, God returned them to the
place He wanted them all along.

Will God have to send a famine into our lives too, or will we
listen the first time and make the right choice?

Thorny Issues

Then Pharaoh, the king of Egypt, gave this order to the Hebrew midwives, Shiphrah and Puah: "When you help the Hebrew women as they give birth, watch as they deliver. If the baby is a boy, kill him; if it is a girl, let her live." But because the midwives feared God, they refused to obey the king's orders. They allowed the boys to live, too.
EXODUS 1:15–17 NLT

The Hebrew midwives faced a terrible choice: Did they obey Pharaoh, or did they do what they knew was right and let the male Hebrew babies live? Their lives and livelihoods could be on the line, but because these women feared God more than Pharaoh, they did the right thing, then lied to Pharaoh when he confronted them about these living boys.

The midwives' situation may remind us of the thorny issues we live with today. There may be no good, honest way out of them. If we are faithful to one, we shortchange another.

God never punished the midwives for lying. Instead, "God was good to the midwives. . . . And because the midwives feared God, he gave them families of their own" (vv. 20–21 NLT). They had balanced the honor they owed the king with the obedience due to God and got it right. No doubt these women had prayed diligently about their actions and discovered that saving many lives was the most critical need. Then they probably asked forgiveness for their lack of truth.

We may know the scriptures and still struggle. But as God led Shiphrah and Puah in the right way, He can lead us too.

Wisdom's Source

Fear of the LORD is the foundation of wisdom.
Knowledge of the Holy One results in good judgment.
PROVERBS 9:10 NLT

What's the basis of good decision-making? Is it growing up in a good family? Getting the best education? Having a good job? Perhaps you feel as if lacking any of these has impeded your ability to make good choices. *If only I'd_____, I might have had a better chance at making good choices,* you may tell yourself.

That simply isn't true. Wisdom doesn't come from this failed world. You can pick up scraps of it from people, but often you'll get a mix of good and bad information. Even the best and most well-meaning folks may not be able to pass on great advice simply because they aren't the source of the best and deepest wisdom. And often you'll hear such conflicting opinions from people that you'll feel more confused than ever. Wisdom is a scarce commodity in this world.

Good advice doesn't necessarily come from good experience, learning the right things, or being in the right place at the right time. But it always comes from God. And the better we know God, the more we can experience His wisdom and make it a part of our lives.

Want to make good decisions? Then drink deep of the wisdom of God. Read His Word and seek to obey what you find there. Draw close to Him through prayer, and commune with others who love Him. For the more you know Jesus, the more your life will be infused with His incomparable wisdom.

Quiet Spirit

If your boss is angry at you, don't quit!
A quiet spirit can overcome even great mistakes.
ECCLESIASTES 10:4 NLT

*E*veryone makes mistakes. No one is perfect on the job or in any other part of life. But how we respond to our own failures can make a huge difference.

If someone in authority—your boss or anyone else—is irked at you, how do you react? Do you shoot back with bitter words, stored up for a long time because you've kept quiet over many grievances? Or do you take a quieter approach?

Will you simply roll over and give up, quitting or becoming even more silent in case you make another mistake? Not speaking out when you really need to could bottle up a collection of nasty grievances that never disappear and never get resolved. When they finally come to a head, will you throw in the towel or boil with revenge?

One way to cultivate a quiet spirit is to keep grievances small. Instead of waiting until you're a kettle on the boil, filled with so many issues you just have to spurt hot water all over everyone, speak to your boss when you only have one issue to deal with. That means you'll probably remain calmer, and you're both more likely to be able to successfully deal with a single issue than a mishmash of problems.

Great mistakes don't need to be perceived as failures, just issues that need to be worked on with a quiet spirit.

Something Important

Pray without ceasing
1 Thessalonians 5:17 KJV

Life-changing troubles staring you in the face? Where do you turn for help?

It's good to talk to some people who might be able to help you with whatever it is you need advice on. But sometimes we spend a lot of time complaining to our friends but slack off in the prayer department. It just feels easier to talk to people than to God.

On occasion, we may even give the nod to God then move on to make our own choices, totally disconnected from His opinion. Proudly using our own intelligence and experience, we head off in a new direction. That's not to say we don't have smarts and knowledge, but how much better, as we start thinking of a new idea or thorny issue, to bring it consistently to God in prayer? To listen for His voice on how we should act and treat others? Tough decisions become easier when the Spirit controls them. What seems like an easy decision may take a new direction when we've sought the counsel of our Lord.

At the end of the day, the advice we most need comes from God. Only He knows the best answer for everything in our lives. After all, isn't He all-knowing and all-powerful? Isn't that a thousand times better than a moment of comfort?

God's input on our decisions can head us in the right direction and help us make even better choices. But unless we ask, we're likely to miss out on something important.

Biblical Support Network

Dear brothers and sisters, if another believer is overcome by some sin, you who are godly should gently and humbly help that person back onto the right path. And be careful not to fall into the same temptation yourself.

GALATIANS 6:1 NLT

ometimes the decisions we're called on to make aren't about our life choices but those of people around us. It's not hard to have someone in your life who has headed off in the wrong direction. The hard part is knowing what you should or shouldn't do about it.

We might want to be like ostriches and ignore another's sin. It's none of my business, we tell ourselves. And certainly that's true if all we want to do is unhelpfully heap condemnation on a sinner.

But the Bible doesn't command us just to step aside and let others wallow in trouble. The church should be a caring place where people help, not a collection of people who stand by and helplessly watch others struggle.

Gently, other Christians need to offer help. Maybe your part will be to tenderly confront the person about sin—or maybe you'll simply need to pray for that hurting soul. God leads each Christian to know what's necessary.

But this verse does not end with help; it ends with a warning. Some may have to become so involved that temptation is a risk. That's why they need to go carefully, and those who pray should pray for everyone involved. But no one needs to fall when God works through His biblical support network.

Goodness and Love?

Surely your goodness and love will follow me all the days of my life, and I will dwell in the house of the LORD forever.

PSALM 23:6 NIV

As tough decisions make an appearance, we may not feel the goodness and love this verse mentions. Stress and doubt may be the most common elements in our lives, and we may begin to worry about where God's goodness and love disappeared to.

Surely there were times in his life when psalmist David didn't feel the love. When Saul wanted to kill him, David had to flee and live in caves. Though Jonathan had David's back in Saul's court, these friends didn't get to spend time together, and Jonathan's efforts to gain David favor with his father weren't very successful.

Running from Saul didn't give David great parenting skills, and fighting battles didn't win him the role of temple builder—David had his failings in life. But the king still proved the truth of God's promise. Goodness and love (though not personal perfection) followed him lifelong. He left his kingdom, one of the greatest in Israel's history, to his son Solomon, beginning fulfillment of the prophecies concerning the Messiah's kingly lineage.

Goodness and love do not only follow a long-dead king. God offers them to all who make the Lord their Shepherd and walk in His paths. Today may be filled with stress and doubt, but it is not the end of the Christian journey. We end in God's house, forever.

The First Choice

And a certain woman named Lydia, a seller of purple, of the city of Thyatira, which worshipped God, heard us: whose heart the Lord opened, that she attended unto the things which were spoken of Paul. And when she was baptized, and her household, she besought us, saying, If ye have judged me to be faithful to the Lord, come into my house, and abide there.

ACTS 16:14–15 KJV

When Paul came to Europe, a worshipper of God called Lydia listened to his message. This successful businesswoman was a Gentile who had contact with Hellenistic Jews and put faith in God, but she had not gone so far as to break from her heritage and join the synagogue. Lydia probably sat on the fence, attracted to God and ready to give Him some of her life, but uncertain what more to do.

When she heard Paul's message, God opened her heart fully. She made the first choice every believer has to make. Courage no longer eluded her, and her heart was free.

Lydia moved wholeheartedly into her new faith, inviting Paul and his disciples into her home. Though they were pretty much strangers, and Paul was from a land she knew little of, she impetuously made the men an integral part of her household for the length of their ministry in Thyatira, blessing the new church with her hospitality.

Do we sit on the fence, spiritually? Or have we committed ourselves to the Lord who tugs at our hearts? God does not seek doubters, but calls us to give our whole lives to Him.

Heavy Laden

Come unto me, all ye that labour and are
heavy laden, and I will give you rest.
MATTHEW 11:28 KJV

In intense times of challenge, decision-making can become a real burden. As the choices pile up, we feel as if we're lifting one-ton blocks on our backs.

Truly, God didn't design people to carry such heavy loads. We are frail beings, emotionally and physically. It's not hard to get out of balance lifting all the worldly choices we face, to say nothing of simultaneously staying on target spiritually.

Does God load us down with troubles? Some claim nothing bad ever comes from God. But how can any of us tell what is bad in our lives? We've had wonderful things come out of terrible trials. If troubles come into our lives and God uses those dark days to redesign our spirits, is that bad? Down the road, that "bad" event may be something we're thankful for.

But our Lord still never wants us to lift one-ton blocks. If we have a heavy-lifting job, it's only because He offers us help. When labor seems too hard and the load is heavy, we need to recognize our own weakness and come to the ultimate heavy lifter: God Himself. Paul knew this truth when, facing persecution, he declared, "For when I am weak, then I am strong" (2 Corinthians 12:10 NIV).

Handing over our burdens gives us rest—the kind we've been looking for all along.

Brave Decisions

*"We should not make it difficult for the Gentiles who are turning
to God. Instead we should write to them, telling them to
abstain from food polluted by idols, from sexual immorality,
from the meat of strangled animals and from blood."*

ACTS 15:19–20 NIV

Some Pharisaical Jews in the early church expected Gentile
converts to go through the rite of circumcision to prove their
commitment to God.

Not unnaturally, many Gentiles didn't think it was such a great
idea to involve that tender physical part in a faith change—after all,
they were not Jews, and Christ never demanded that circumcision be
applied to non-Jews. Debate on the topic raged back and forth and
threatened to split the fledgling church, so the question came before
a church council at Jerusalem.

If there was ever a question about James's bravery, that issue was
settled on the day the council's judgment came down. Risking the
anger of Christians from his own nation, Jerusalem's leader spoke
the words of these verses and encouraged Gentiles to leave behind
paganism and come to Jesus.

Had James gone with the people of his own nation, the Gospel
message might have stayed largely in Israel, as Gentiles refused to
commit to a faith that both drew them and repelled them. Accepting
the Law's requirement in this instance probably would have led to
additional debates and enforcement of other Old Testament practices
on the new church. Freedom in Christ would have been lost.

James carefully studied the issue, consulted with others, and
made a brave choice. In doing so, he shows us how to make our own
difficult decisions.

Ever Faithful

*But Johanan the son of Kareah, and all the captains of the forces,
took all the remnant of Judah, that were returned from all
nations. . . . So they came into the land of Egypt: for they obeyed
not the voice of the Lord: thus came they even to Tahpanhes.
Then came the word of the Lord unto Jeremiah in Tahpanhes.*
JEREMIAH 43:5, 7–8 KJV

Jeremiah had clearly passed on God's message to Judah: the Jews left in the land after Jerusalem's fall to the Chaldean forces were not to go to Egypt. There was no doubt in God's mind—or the prophet's—about this message, and there was no question that Johanan and his soldiers were not of a mind to listen. The military swept the Jews into Egypt, though Jeremiah had prophesied that going there would lead to disaster.

Jeremiah was a powerful prophet who spoke out freely against the move. For his trouble, he was accused of treason. But despite the mistreatment, Jeremiah chose to go with his people into Egypt. Ever faithful to his mission, he went where God called and no doubt died in the foreign land. Jewish tradition says the prophet was stoned to death.

As with Jeremiah, not everyone we are called to serve will be faithful to God, but, like the prophet, we can still be faithful to the mission He calls us to. Whether we chose to go to Egypt or stay in Judah, we must always do His will.

A Thoughtful Response

*"May God strike me and even kill me if I don't do everything
I can to help David get what the LORD has promised him!
I'm going to take Saul's kingdom and give it to David."*
2 SAMUEL 3:9–10 NLT

bner, powerful army commander to King Saul, threw this threat in the face of Saul's son, Ishbosheth. On his father's death, Abner had made Ishbosheth king of Israel, only to be accused of an illicit relationship with one of Saul's concubines—that was Ishbosheth's way of accusing the commander of having designs on his throne.

Honorable Abner was not going to stand for it. He'd rather change allegiance than have his name wrongly besmirched, and that's just what he did. By the time Ishbosheth backed down, the affronted leader had sent a message to David, offering to help him take the throne.

Saul's son is a good example of bad actions. Instead of confronting Abner, he should have checked out the accusations against the commander and considered his power over the military. If Abner had formed a plot against Ishbosheth, the king had to respond, but with careful planning, not words that warned his opponent and caused the commander to respond in anger.

Before we accuse another of wrongdoing, let's take advantage of this bad example and make certain the facts are right and that our act of opposition is wise. Prayer and planning work better than a rushed, thoughtless response—for us as well as Ishbosheth.

Selflessness Personified

〰〰〰

*"Don't be afraid," Jonathan said. "My father Saul will never get
his hands on you. In fact, you're going to be the next king of Israel,
and I'll be your highest official. Even my father knows it's true."*

1 SAMUEL 23:17 CEV

❧

Not many men would willingly give up a throne so a best
friend could sit on it. But Jonathan stands out in scripture
for his willingness to do just that.

From the time David came to King Saul's court, the two men were
the best of friends. Though he was the king's son and in line for the
throne, Jonathan always seemed to put his friend first. While Saul
repeatedly tried to kill David, Jonathan attempted to bring peace
between the men. All his efforts failed.

It seems hard to believe that, apart from God, anyone could
be so giving. Scripture doesn't tell us if Jonathan was so selfless
concerning the kingdom because God made it clear to him that
this was His plan. Perhaps David confided in his friend the story of
the prophet coming to his family and anointing him king. Jonathan
might have wanted to do God's will, but he still would have been
selflessness personified to do so.

Compared to Jonathan, what has God called us to give up? Time?
Energy? Some money? Few of us have given up as much as Saul's
son just to see a friend succeed. So when God calls us to give to our
friends, let's remember Jonathan's example and do our part graciously.

Good or Better?

Naomi then said to Ruth, "Look, your sister-in-law is going back to her people and to her gods! Why don't you go with her?"
RUTH 1:15 CEV

Naomi knew she would return to her homeland destitute. How could she ask her daughters-in-law to share that lifestyle? Though the famine that had moved her family to Moab had ended and the Lord had provided food for Judah, life still wouldn't be easy. Bravely, the older woman prepared to send Orpah and Ruth back to their families.

Orpah, understanding her logic, turned and went. But Ruth surprised her mother-in-law. Firmly, she refused security and determinedly set out for Judah with Naomi.

So often we focus on Ruth's selflessness. But what of Naomi? Penniless, hopeless, her whole being probably hurt as she turned away her only means of support. Naomi's brain told her that taking those she loved into misery was a poor return for their love, and she tried to turn them back, but how Ruth's willingness to go to Judah must have strengthened the widow's spirit. Yet even then, Naomi tried to turn back her daughter by marriage, pointing out the sense in Orpah's decision.

Selfless Naomi made a hard choice, but when she was on the brink of despair, God put promise in her future through one loving woman. The widow's selfless choice turned her hopelessness into a brighter future.

Like Naomi, when we make selfless choices, God watches out for us. Where we seek to do good, He may put something even better in our lives.

Forgiven?

[Abraham asked,] "Wouldn't you spare the city if there are only fifty good people in it? You surely wouldn't let them be killed when you destroy the evil ones. You are the judge of all the earth, and you do what is right."
GENESIS 18:24–25 CEV

When God confided to Abraham that He planned to destroy the city of Sodom, the prophet's mind flew to his nephew, Lot, who lived there. Immediately, he began testing the waters with God to see if his family would be saved.

Abraham's concern is a bit surprising. Lot had taken the best of the Promised Land when the two men had to split it for the sake of peace. Abraham allowed his nephew first choice, and instead of making an even split, greedy Lot grabbed the richest pasturelands. But the "best" land turned out not to be best after all, since sinful Sodom came with this land grant.

Having made his agreement, Abraham lived by it without bitterness and even came to Lot's rescue when Sodom was attacked. Now, as God planned a more certain destruction of the city, the prophet again came to his nephew's aid.

Trusting in God's promise that he would never lack for land (Genesis 13:15–16), the prophet didn't simply avoid the wrongdoer but lived in active peace with him. Though they didn't interact daily, Abraham still cared.

Not all of our relationships will be perfect, just as Abraham's weren't. But will we hold that grudge or, like Abraham, offer forgiveness?

Ultimate Victory

David spoke to Ittai and said, "You're a foreigner from the town of Gath. You don't have to leave with us. Go back and join the new king! You haven't been with me very long, so why should you have to follow me, when I don't even know where I'm going? Take your soldiers and go back. I pray that the Lord will be kind and faithful to you." Ittai answered, "Your Majesty, just as surely as you and the Lord live, I will go where you go, no matter if it costs me my life."
2 SAMUEL 15:19–21 CEV

*D*isplaced from his capital by his rebellious son, Absalom, David left Jerusalem with his soldiers. As his last men passed the gates, thoughts of days past must have come to the king's mind. These six hundred warriors had followed him from Gath, where David had served a pagan king while Saul sought his life. This battle for Israel's throne was not Commander Ittai's or his men's.

But when David tried to turn Ittai back, the commander freely offered his life for his chosen king. For his faithfulness, David made him one of his three top commanders in the battles that ensued. Ittai had chosen wisely, for, using the commander from Gath's leadership and the courage of his men, David quickly overthrew Absalom.

When our cause seems conquered, do we desert our chosen king? Or, like Ittai, will we see the ultimate victory ahead and remain faithful to Him for the long haul?

Setting Things Right

Judah recognized them immediately and said, "She is more righteous than I am, because I didn't arrange for her to marry my son Shelah." And Judah never slept with Tamar again.

GENESIS 38:26 NLT

Eating humble pie, especially spiritually, has to be one of the hardest decisions we make, and it hardly makes it easier when the person who hands us the pie also has a less-than-perfect track record.

That's just the situation Judah was in. His daughter-in-law, who had outlived two of his sons, was pregnant out of wedlock.

"Burn her!" Judah commanded, acting as both judge and jury.

That's when the story changes. Tamar had a little secret—and so did Judah. Unable to convince Judah to provide for her by letting her marry his third son, Tamar had set a trap for her father-in-law; dressing as a prostitute, she put herself in his path. Judah took advantage of her sexual favors. It's a good thing Tamar was thoughtful about her plan, or she would have been dead, but she had made him give her his seal and staff, proof that he had been intimate with her.

When she proved that he had been the man, her father-in-law had no other option than to recognize his own failure and forgive her.

Judah isn't the only one who has had to eat that humble pie. Though we may not have to admit to such a sensational sin, we sometimes have to backtrack too. May we be as quick as Judah to admit our wrongs and set them right.

Closed Door

"So fear the LORD and serve him wholeheartedly. . . .
Serve the LORD alone. But if you refuse to serve the LORD,
then choose today whom you will serve. . . . But as for
me and my family, we will serve the LORD."
JOSHUA 24:14–15 NLT

*J*oshua ended his ministry to God's people with a reminder of God's faithfulness to His nation: He had brought them into a Promised Land filled with many tribes and enabled them to conquer the land. With this reminder, the prophet pointed out that it was time for the people to remember their side of the covenant.

Israel's devotion to God was not to be halfhearted or partial. He didn't expect them to serve Him when it was convenient while worshipping pagan deities in crisis times. Either they would serve Him or choose another, but each person had to make a decision who their Lord was. They could serve the Lord or the ancient gods of their forefathers or even the Amorite gods, whose people they had conquered. But they couldn't serve more than one.

God is a jealous God: He will not take our leftover worship. Just like the people of Israel, we either choose to serve Him or give our allegiance to another. But the option of serving Him and another is a closed door.

Have you made a conscious decision about whom you will serve? If not, now is a perfect decision time.

Follow the Lord!

*"If my people would only listen to me, if Israel would only
follow my ways. . .you would be fed with the finest of wheat;
with honey from the rock I would satisfy you."*

PSALM 81:13, 16 NIV

"ollow the Lord." You've probably heard that advice, however
phrased, from the pulpit or from friends you've shared your
troubles with.

If only it were that easy, you may have thought. *Such simplistic
advice doesn't take into account all the challenges involved.* You may
have been tempted to discount the advice, faulting it as being trite
and overly obvious.

But the people who pass on that well-meaning, but perhaps
irritating, counsel are only giving you God's advice, repeated over
and over in His Word. Hearing it may be hard, but this simple truth
still is the sole path to blessing: nothing good comes into our lives
when we ignore God's will and way.

Perhaps the idea would have more appeal if those advisers also
quoted verse 16. God not only asks us to obey, but He also promises
that following His commands brings us satisfaction. Promises of
blessings—and even more, the blessings themselves at work in our
lives—help us understand the good God wants us to enjoy.

So no matter what rock you are trying to split, remember that
some honey will come out of it. It may not be that sticky sweetener,
but blessings come to your life when you follow Him faithfully.
Satisfaction guaranteed!

Trust for in Between

"Naked I came from my mother's womb, and naked
I will depart. The LORD gave and the LORD has taken
away; may the name of the LORD be praised."
JOB 1:21 NIV

eally, that's Job's response to loss? we may wonder. His words, spoken after losing almost everything he owned and loved, are pretty stunning. In the middle of such a desperate situation, what's he doing *praising* God? Doesn't he know he's in trouble?

Job is an amazing man; perhaps that's why God knew he could safely send Satan to test him. Whatever the evil one did, Job had his priorities straight: everything wealthy Job had belonged to God, and no matter what happened, praise was due Him.

Perhaps Job realized that God had been good the day before disaster fell on him, and His nature hadn't changed, no matter what happened. God never changes, no matter how wild the world gets or how many mistakes and sins are part of our lives. Both coming into the world and leaving it with nothing show our complete dependence on Him, so if God wanted Job to be naked in the middle of his life, it was simply a link between beginning and end.

That's trust.

When our decision-making seems to have stripped us of everything, like Job, we still have God. He brought us into the world and will be with us as we leave it. Can't we trust Him with everything in between?

Never Give Up

Mary said, "I am the Lord's servant!
Let it happen as you have said." And the angel left her.

LUKE 1:38 CEV

Though she must have been astonished at the news the angel brought her, Mary didn't hem and haw about the prospect of bearing the Messiah. Recognizing what an honor God had done her, she immediately declared her willingness to serve.

Later, that response may have seemed a bit impulsive as she wondered what Joseph would think of a pregnancy he'd had no part in. And when he decided to quietly end their betrothal, she must have felt bereft. Though her cousin Elizabeth supported her, knowing what God had done, others weren't so understanding. Following through on that first quick commitment turned out to be a real test of Mary's faith. Every day of her life from that moment on, Mary had to deal with the results of her obedience to God. She came through with flying colors. But that doesn't mean it was easy for her, though God always faithfully supported her.

Mary wasn't the only one to quickly commit to something, only to have issues come up later. Faith is a day-by-day event. Committing to following God's will means we agree to hang in there when the going gets tough and when unexpected troubles come up. We never give up.

But no matter what they face, God's always with His servants. He never fails those with obedient, willing hearts. He too never gives up.

Large Job

*When Joseph woke up, he did as the angel of the Lord
commanded and took Mary as his wife.*
MATTHEW 1:24 NLT

Though Joseph had nearly decided not to marry Mary, divine confirmation of her innocence changed his mind. Hardly knowing what to expect, the carpenter committed to their unusual relationship. Though he must have felt relief that she had not betrayed him, he must also have understood that the task ahead was large. Only a man of great character and faith could have raised God's Son.

Joseph's new family included a Son unlike any the world had seen before. Raising God's Son had to have been the most intimidating job anyone has ever faced. Yet he bravely took the job God offered.

It's doubtful that Joseph could ever have imagined the job God had for him. As a child, it's doubtful he dreamed of being the Messiah's earthly father. Who even knew there was such a spiritual job description? And there was no how-to book for being Jesus' father. The only way Joseph had an inkling about what to do was through the support he no doubt received through prayer and communion with the Lord.

God may bring large jobs into our lives too—those that stretch our abilities, draw out our weaknesses, and pull us in unexpected directions. Though not as unusual as Joseph's call, they may take every bit of our spiritual and physical strength. Will we put our lives at God's disposal?

One Day at a Time

"So don't worry about tomorrow, for tomorrow will bring its own worries. Today's trouble is enough for today."
MATTHEW 6:34 NLT

eally good decisions are never made out of worry, because when intense concern for what lies ahead clouds our minds, we're likely to have short-term vision. We're myopic when we make a choice based on only immediate needs.

In an insecure world, it's hard to look up and see hope. As we try to patch together a more perfect life, we're usually blind to the good things that could lie ahead. But God has the long-term vision we need, for He knows our future and His plans for it. While we envision a straight path that goes over few hills, He may have mountains for us to climb. But if we knew those mountains lay ahead, how discouraged we would become, so He doesn't let us see them ahead of time.

God knows our frailty and our tendency to worry, and He knows we can't improve anything with our concern. So instead, He encourages us to keep our eyes focused on what we can do: living this day to the fullest, in obedience to Him.

You won't be able to change troubles that lie ahead, so do what you can to plan for the immediate future, and leave it to God to plan the years that lie ahead. Live well one day at a time, and your future will end up being bright too.

The Weakness of Pride

*[Naaman's servants said,] "If the prophet had told you to do
something very difficult, wouldn't you have done it? So you should
certainly obey him when he says simply, 'Go and wash and be cured!'"
So Naaman went down to the Jordan River and dipped himself seven
times, as the man of God had instructed him. And his skin became
as healthy as the skin of a young child, and he was healed!*

2 KINGS 5:13–14 NLT

Naaman wasn't at all pleased with the prophet Elisha. It didn't
suit the commander of Aram's army that the prophet didn't
treat him as an important guest, but when Elisha told him to bathe
in the Jordan River to heal his leprosy, the commander lost it. Weren't
the rivers in his homeland good enough, and couldn't any prophet
worth his salt have simply waved a hand over him and cured him?

Naaman's servants had to talk Naaman off the ledge. They simply
pointed out that a bath in a river wasn't a particularly hard thing
to do. He wanted to be rid of his leprosy, didn't he? And no one in
Aram had that power.

Proud Naaman rethought his plan and humbly went down to
the river. After dipping himself in seven times, he found his skin
smooth and clean.

Does pride come between us and good decision-making? Like
Naaman, we will work against our own best interests if we let that
happen. The Bible warns in Proverbs 16:18 (NLT): "Pride goes before
destruction, and haughtiness before a fall." Let's take that warning
seriously.

Perfect Justice

Do not say, "I'll pay you back for this wrong!"
Wait for the LORD, and he will avenge you.
PROVERBS 20:22 NIV

ot getting payback, forgiving someone who hurt us and isn't sorry—those ideas go against the grain. After all, isn't making another person pay for a sin justice? How can we watch others get away with serious wrongs and not seethe inside for years to come?

Everyone gets wronged at some time, and no matter how it comes, it hurts. If we listen to our sinful selves, we'll probably want to zip back with retaliation. With words or actions we know God doesn't approve of, we can try to even the score. But hours or days later, we still feel the pain. Nothing made our loss right, and now we simply feel guilty for our own nasty actions. Retaliation just doesn't work the way we think it should because it never really solves the problem.

So God offers us a better option: let Him do the avenging. And that's the perfect response, both because we do not sin and because God is in charge of our lives and the other person's. Our heavenly Father knows the person who offended us as well as He knows us. His actions are just and perfect in a way ours never could be.

Knowing that, are we willing to let Him establish a perfect justice, or do we really want to take it back into our own hands?

Every Day

I have set before you life and death, blessings and curses.
Now choose life, so that you and your children may live
and that you may love the LORD your God, listen to his voice,
and hold fast to him. For the LORD is your life.
DEUTERONOMY 30:19–20 NIV

*M*oses set a choice before God's people: they could have life with God or death by following after pagan deities.

The people he spoke to had crossed the Red Sea in the wake of God's miracle. They had been fed manna in the desert and had seen God's faithfulness as He led them to the Promised Land. Their parents had turned away from the land once, and for forty years He kept them all moving but safe, while surrounded by enemies. These people had experienced God's blessings and known His law.

There shouldn't have been a need to choose, right? How could God have made His presence clearer than the fire by night and the cloud by day that led their families out of Egypt? Was there really any question that they would be obedient?

Yes. For just as God has done great things in our lives and we have fallen away from Him, the Israelites would slip away from knowledge and trust in their Lord. Following God is not a matter of witnessing miracles or making a single, lifelong choice; it's an everyday habit of decision-making that keeps us close to Him.

Today, will you choose life?

Everlasting Way

Search me, God, and know my heart; test me and know my anxious thoughts. See if there is any offensive way in me, and lead me in the way everlasting.
PSALM 139:23–24 NIV

Decision-making often goes hand in hand with anxiety. Will we make the right choice or fall for an option we'll regret for years? We have no way of knowing the future, and in our humanity, we tend to worry when we don't see a clear, straight path lying in front of us.

But anxiety isn't a part of God's design for our lives. He has a better idea. Instead of having us constantly focus on all the things we don't know, things that could fill at least a large book, He wants us to keep our eyes on Him, because, no matter what we can't see, we can always trust that He knows what lies ahead and what we need to do to come through well.

If we get off track with our choices, we can't blame it on God. He doesn't want to see us head off in the wrong direction, and He encourages us to seek His ways. But neither is He a tyrant who forces us in a certain direction. If we rebelliously refuse the way His Word points us or we simply never seek His guidance, He'll let us reap what we have sown. Next time, we may check with Him first.

God wants us to avoid offending Him and follow in His everlasting way. But the choice is all up to us. Will we go in the everlasting way?

The Best Wisdom

I cry out to the LORD; I plead for the LORD's mercy.
I pour out my complaints before him and tell him all my troubles.
PSALM 142:1–2 NLT

Need someone to tell your decision-making troubles to? Share them with God. Whether you've made a bad choice or have been offended by someone else because you made a right one, God always wants to hear your side of the story.

Telling our woes to God means we never have to worry about someone not understanding or passing on a word of gossip to a third party. God may encourage us to make things right with someone we've wronged, but He will never go to that person and share our confidences. And no human can give us better advice than He can.

That doesn't mean we shouldn't ask for wisdom from strong Christians—we should do just that, because Proverbs 19:20 (KJV) says: "Hear counsel, and receive instruction, that thou mayest be wise in thy latter end." But our first and strongest resource is God. Before we go to others, if we go to God, our problem may find a quick solution. And we still have the option of receiving wise advice from humans.

Don't think you will "worry" God with your troubles. He knows you have them and cares more deeply than you'd imagine. He is your loving Father, who reaches His hand down to you. Ask the Merciful One for help every day, and connect to the best wisdom on earth.

Goodness and Mercy

Answer me, LORD, out of the goodness of your love;
in your great mercy turn to me.

PSALM 69:16 NIV

oodness and mercy, lifelong. What good news that is to our aching hearts and spirits!

But do we let goodness and mercy stand to the side when we make decisions about other people? Perhaps we frequently expect others to toe the line.

Though that attitude may seem just, it isn't very compassionate. The deep joy we find in God's goodness and mercy is bound up in His forgiveness—something we can pass on.

God could have been just toward His failed people. Justice would have required repayment for sin, and we all would have spent eternity cast out of heaven. God would have been perfectly right in doing that. But God is not simply just; He is good and merciful too. So instead of making us toe the line, He gave us a path to forgiveness: Jesus. When we least deserved it, He offered us all that we could not do for ourselves.

That doesn't mean we shouldn't have standards or that we should let people steamroll right over us, but it does mean there should be more than justice in our hearts. When others could be touched by a gentle word or action, it's up to us to remember the One who introduced those qualities into our lives.

When we decide to follow God in giving love and mercy, we will have made the right choice.

Faithful

*"Our God whom we serve is able to deliver us from the burning
fiery furnace, and He will deliver us from your hand, O king.
But if not, let it be known to you, O king, that we do not serve your
gods, nor will we worship the gold image which you have set up."*
DANIEL 3:17–18 NKJV

Imagine having to make the choice to say these words to a
ruler you refused to worship, knowing that he might condemn
you to the hottest part of the fire. For brave and faithful Shadrach,
Meshach, and Abednego, serving God meant more than life itself.
They would be faithful, no matter the cost.

The angry ruler put their faith to the test when he did just what
might be expected. Nebuchadnezzar had a fire heated to seven times
its usual strength, and his men threw the Hebrews in. So hot were
the flames that the soldiers who threw them in died. But the three
faith-filled men, who had lifted up their situation to their Savior,
were not deserted. A fourth man, "like the Son of God" (v. 25 NKJV),
protected them, and when they came out of the fire, their clothes
didn't even smell smoky.

Though He may not do it often, God also asks us to stand up
for our faith. Whether we fear for our lives, our livelihoods, or just
our good names, we will be put to the test. Can we trust that God
will be there for us, no matter what is brought against us? What
will we say?

When we're faithful, He will be sure to show us He is too.

Thanks-and-Praise Party

*Giving thanks to the Father who has qualified us to be
partakers of the inheritance of the saints in the light.*
COLOSSIANS 1:12 NKJV

When our decision-making process works out well, do we thank God for His wisdom that guided us to making a strong choice? Or do we applaud our own abilities and ignore the guidance that put us in the best decision-making mode?

Often our borrowed wisdom comes from God's Word, a powerful sermon we've heard, or even just the advice of a believing friend. However it happens, when we hear the Word's truth, it is God's message of wisdom to us. It's as if He has grabbed our hands and said, "Go in this direction." We listen, and our lives are blessed.

Other times, we make decisions based on our history as Christians. We have stored up scripture in our hearts to the point where a biblical reaction feels natural. When we make wise choices, they are still not based on our own power; God has implanted principles in our lives that affect our actions, and the glory still belongs to Him.

It's easy to get so caught up in the need to make decisions that we become thankless. Though we still love God, we can carelessly fail to open our mouths in appreciation.

This might be a good moment to thoughtfully remember all the choices God has helped us with and throw a thanks-and-praise party. We don't want to be His thankless children!

Senseless?

The LORD said, "Hosea, Israel has betrayed me like an
unfaithful wife. Marry such a woman and have children by her."
HOSEA 1:2 CEV

his must have been one of those "God, what are You thinking?"
moments for Hosea. Marry a harlot? How could God ask him
to do that?

Yet when God commanded Hosea, he chose to obey. And this
wasn't a marriage in name only—the couple had three children
before his wife, Gomer, tired of marriage and became unfaithful to
the prophet.

Following her unfaithfulness, God called the prophet to bring
Gomer home again. "Then the LORD said to me, 'Go and love your
wife again, even though she commits adultery with another lover.
This will illustrate that the LORD still loves Israel, even though
the people have turned to other gods and love to worship them'"
(Hosea 3:1 NLT). Having her around must have been like biting on
a sore tooth, but Hosea obeyed that command and God's direction
to love her.

Hosea lived out a picture of the love God had for His faithless
people, Israel. Though their betrayal hurt Him as personally as a
husband betrayed by his wife, God would not give up on them.

Has God called you to do something that doesn't seem to make
solid sense? He has a purpose for those seemingly senseless commands. Perhaps you, like Hosea, will become a powerful example to
others of the forgiveness that only comes through Him.

Blessings Beyond Money

*"Should people cheat God? Yet you. . .have cheated me of the
tithes and offerings due to me. . . . Bring all the tithes into the
storehouse. . . . If you do," says the LORD of Heaven's Armies,
"I will open the windows of heaven for you. I will pour
out a blessing so great you won't have enough room
to take it in! Try it! Put me to the test!"*
MALACHI 3:8, 10 NLT

One thing we make daily decisions about is money. Whether it's paying bills or supporting our churches, we all write checks, submit payments online, or give others cash.

Money's one of the easiest things to think we own, and many of us get really touchy when someone else tries to put a hand in our pockets. That's fine if they're trying to do something dishonest.

But when God puts a hand in our pockets to remind us that we should tithe, that's another matter. Because everything we own, down to the last cent, is really His. Who gave us that job or those savings? Who can give us more—or withhold money from us entirely? Who can provide for us in ways that don't require one red cent?

When God asks us to give, it's not a one-way street. Those who give will also receive. Maybe it won't be a bigger house, but it might be more peace in our lives or spiritual growth or a million other things.

Let's use our money wisely.

Good Stewards

*And God blessed them, and God said unto them, Be fruitful,
and multiply, and replenish the earth, and subdue it:
and have dominion over the fish of the sea, and over the
fowl of the air, and over every living thing
that moveth upon the earth.*

GENESIS 1:28 KJV

G od threw the planets into space, then took one and carefully provided it with all that was necessary for life—water, vegetation, trees, air. Then within this lovely landscape, He created animals and humans to enjoy His beautiful creation. Pleased, He declared it all good.

But even as man looks out over this beautiful land and views beautiful birds flying above it, he seeks to change it. Before long, beautiful forests are cut down to make room for houses. The animals are in the way, so man kills them or forces them to move to less beneficent lands. With the changes in the landscape, life becomes less good for man and beast. In time, factories that pop up pollute the land, and what was once so good seems good no more.

Some choices we make do not simply affect our lives. A few influence the entire globe we live on. Let's remember that God has made us stewards of His land, not owners. How we use this greatest gift He's given us can bring blessing or disaster.

Will we replenish God's earth or simply work toward our own gain?

Animal Rights and Wrongs

The godly care for their animals,
but the wicked are always cruel.
PROVERBS 12:10 NLT

"It's only an animal," you often hear people say dismissively when they are less than concerned about a beast's life. But that's not the attitude of God, who created every one of them and watches over them. He who sees even the sparrows fall has a vested interest in all His creation.

How a human treats animals is one way to tell where her true heart is. Those with hearts that are soft toward God treat furry and feathered animals with kindness and gentleness. It's a kind of thermometer that shows internal spiritual temperature. Is it any surprise that law enforcement discovered those who abuse animals often abuse humans too? It doesn't make a difference if the victim is a plow horse that helps ready the field for planting or if it's a pet dog, cat, or bird, animal cruelty matters to God.

When we make decisions to be kind to those who cannot speak for themselves and are largely helpless in our hands, we treat them the way our heavenly Father wants us to treat His whole creation—human and animal.

See that dog left out in the cold all night with no shelter? Would Jesus pass by without a care? Or would He show concern for both man and beast and see that both were made right?

Ultimate Blessing

Then the LORD asked Satan, "Have you noticed my servant Job?
He is the finest man in all the earth. He is blameless—a man
of complete integrity. He fears God and stays away from evil."

JOB 1:8 NLT

Job, as John Gill comments, "was upright in his walk and conversation before God, and also before men; upright in all his dealings and concerns with them, in every relation he stood, in every office and character he bore." With all these qualities, rooted in his faith, he led what we would call a blessed life. He had wealth, a happy family, everything a man could need.

But God was about to bless him more, with a trial that would shake his world to its foundations.

Faithful Job made all the right decisions. He'd honored God, rigorously made sacrifices for his whole family, and treated his neighbors with respect. No one had a complaint against him, but suddenly Job's world fell apart.

Where had he gone wrong? Nowhere.

God simply wanted to deepen Job's understanding of Himself. By the end of the book, Job understood his own small nature and God's great one.

Though he lost so much, Job lost nothing. Following his trials, God blessed His child even more than before (Job 42:12). Former blessings paled before God's final outpouring of good things. But the greatest blessing was deeper knowledge of the Lord.

We too can make the right choices—at least as right as we know how to—and still end up in a difficult spot. Maybe God is preparing us for His ultimate blessing.

Follow Him

Jesus. . .saw a tax collector named Levi sitting at his tax collector's booth. "Follow me and be my disciple," Jesus said to him. So Levi got up, left everything, and followed him.
LUKE 5:27–28 NLT

Levi made a good, if dishonest, living, pressing his fellow Jews to pay taxes to Rome. There were drawbacks, of course. Being called a traitor and being treated as an outcast was no fun, but it seemed a small price to pay for wealth. Maybe Levi wasn't a very social person anyway. And he could always pay back irritating fellow Jews by upping their taxes.

Levi made terrible choices that cut him off from his neighbors. As a tax collector, he wasn't allowed in the synagogue. Nothing seemed more unlikely than a popular young preacher eating at his home. But that's just where Jesus dined one night, with all of Levi's friends—other tax collectors and sinners.

Happily, Jesus wasn't as concerned with looks as the critical Pharisees were—He was interested in the hearts of those men who were so far from God. He wanted to turn their lives around and forgive their bad choices. He certainly did that with Gospel writer Levi, later called Matthew.

Levi isn't the only one whose choices can make a one-hundred-and-eighty-degree turn. God does that all the time for anyone willing to get up and follow Him. So which direction are you heading in?

Command Performance

Instead, Jonah ran from the LORD. He went to the seaport of Joppa and bought a ticket on a ship that was going to Spain. Then he got on the ship and sailed away to escape.

JONAH 1:3 CEV

"Go to Nineveh," God told the prophet Jonah. "I have some preaching for you to do there."

Jonah didn't say a word. He didn't have to, for his actions spoke more loudly than his mouth could. He ran to the port of Joppa and boarded a ship headed far out in the opposite direction. It wasn't that he wanted to visit Spain's balmy beaches; Jonah just wanted to get as far away as possible from a task he hated. Nineveh was the capital of Assyria, a violent and powerful nation and Israel's enemy.

Silly Jonah. How could he have hoped to escape God? Wasn't he a prophet? Didn't he understand the powerful Lord he served?

We can understand the prophet's aversion to preaching God's love to his enemies. The ruins of Nineveh lie across the Tigris River from modern-day Mosul, in Iraq. How many American missionaries would jump at the opportunity to minister there?

After he'd spent some time in a fish belly, Jonah got the idea that there were no other options for him. He went and did a fine job.

Some decisions God leaves to His people. Others are command performances. Have we been called to play before the King? Will we go?

Never Lost

When people do not accept divine guidance,
they run wild. But whoever obeys the law is joyful.
PROVERBS 29:18 NLT

We all have some unspoken motivation that drives our decision-making. Are we looking out for number one? Avid about changing the world? Committed to obeying God? Something moves us to act the way we do.

Without God's guidance, we go off in the wrong direction. So many false hopes call us into sin. We lack the GPS to guide us in the right direction, and we can end up lost and wandering hopelessly.

God knows where humans end up without Him, and that's why He sent prophets and apostles to write the long Book that provides the detailed map we need to point us in the right direction—His direction. You won't find it on a compass—there's no point marked "God" there. But once Jesus is in your heart, you will find yourself continually gravitating toward Him.

But that doesn't happen automatically. To follow our Lord, we need to know what's written in the Book He prepared just for us. We need to read it, commit its commands to memory, and obey it. Knowing the words but ignoring them will get us nowhere.

When we follow His compass, we'll have a vision for our lives and knowledge of where we're going. Traveling in His direction, we are never lost or hopeless.

Still Grieving?

Now the LORD said to Samuel, "You have mourned long enough
for Saul. I have rejected him as king of Israel, so fill your flask
with olive oil and go to Bethlehem. Find a man named Jesse who
lives there, for I have selected one of his sons to be my king."
1 SAMUEL 16:1 NLT

After God anointed Saul as king of Israel, the king went in his
own direction, disobeying God's specific instructions about
destroying the Amalekites and all they owned. Greedy Saul spared
King Agag and the best of that nation's cattle. In that choice, he ran
counter to God and lost his kingdom.

This spiritual failure struck the prophet Samuel hard. Sadly, he
had to tell Saul that God would not forgive him. But seemingly, the
prophet hoped God would somehow turn things around, and Saul
could become the king God meant him to be.

That's when the Lord spoke these words to Samuel, telling him
to let the past go and take action. God had another king in mind
and sent the prophet to anoint one of Jesse's sons, David.

Occasionally, God calls us to leave the past behind and move
ahead, though we are still grieving. When that happens, we may
move more slowly than usual, but we can go forward in hope. As
with Samuel, God has a good plan, though we may not see it.

David, whom Samuel never wanted to take Saul's place, became
a man after God's own heart (Acts 13:22), forefather of His Messiah.

Wise Choices?

This is what he said: Who does this David think he is?
That son of Jesse is just one more slave on the run from his master,
and there are too many of them these days. What makes you
think I would take my bread, my water, and the meat that
I've had cooked for my own servants and give it to you?
Besides, I'm not sure that David sent you!
1 SAMUEL 25:10–11 CEV

*I*f you had a wolf in your backyard, would you decide to tease it? That's about what Nabal did when David sent men to ask for help from this wealthy landowner whose property God's anointed king had protected during his battles with King Saul. The landowner's rude response was like poking a stick at a wolf just out of curiosity. And make no mistake, David was as dangerous as any wild canid.

Nabal came incredibly close to having his backyard annihilated.

Nabal's bad decision was two-fold: first, he was greedy and probably would never have given aid to David under any circumstances; second, he intentionally insulted the most powerful man in the neighborhood. Truly, his name, which means "fool," aptly described him.

Are we in danger of making split-second, self-serving, and unwise decisions? Then let's remember Nabal and the end he would have come to had his wife, Abigail, not stepped in and given David what he requested. Before we snap out an unwise response, let's send a prayer upward.

God's Still Working

*Later, when the boy was older, his mother brought him back
to Pharaoh's daughter, who adopted him as her own son.
The princess named him Moses, for she explained,
"I lifted him out of the water."*

EXODUS 2:10 NLT

ometimes God uses the choices of the most unexpected people to work His will in the lives of believers. They don't have to be Christians or even sympathetic to Christianity or God's people. When God wants to work through someone, it can happen in an instant.

Moses' mother, desperate to save her son, had put the tiny baby in a tar-and-pitch-covered basket and floated him out on the Nile River. She hoped someone would find the child and save him. But would she have imagined that Pharaoh's daughter would take him in? It would have seemed a long shot, but, with God leading, that's just what happened.

His mother had the joy of raising him. Then when the child had grown a bit, he entered the household of Pharaoh's daughter, where Moses gained contact with the court—the place he would eventually bring God's message. God used one desperate woman's actions to bring about His larger goals.

Even when our lives seem out of control, utterly confused, and hopeless, and our choices pointless, God may still be working some great thing. When we risk it all, like Moses' mom, we can be sure the heavenly arms are still below us, waiting to catch us.

Isn't that what faith is?

Less Painful

When Haman entered the room, the king asked him,
"What should I do for a man I want to honor?"
Haman was sure that he was the one the
king wanted to honor.
ESTHER 6:6 CEV

For those of us who know the whole story of Haman, this moment is rather comical. Hearing that the king wanted to honor someone, this proud man assumed that, naturally, it had to be himself. He thought the king was asking, "What would you like me to do for you?" So Haman suggested that he be paraded in front of the city in the king's robes and on one of his horses.

Imagine his shock when the king called on Haman to do this for his enemy, Mordecai. Mordecai probably couldn't have cared less about being so publicly honored. But to Haman, it was an unbearably painful day, glorifying the man he hated.

Haman's foolishness is a fairly amusing warning against pride. But we've all been in enough similar situations that we can hurt for the wicked man just a little—and hope we'd never put ourselves in a position of such embarrassment.

May our own self-opinions be less in line with Haman's thinking and more in line with God's: "All those who exalt themselves will be humbled, and those who humble themselves will be exalted" (Luke 14:11 NIV). When God exalts us, we'll feel nothing but joy.

Turn Again

Now Peter was sitting out in the courtyard, and a servant girl came to him. "You also were with Jesus of Galilee," she said. But he denied it before them all. "I don't know what you're talking about," he said.

MATTHEW 26:69–70 NIV

ig, brave Peter. Who would have ever thought this brash man of faith would turn away from the Master? Hadn't he left his profitable fishing business to go on the road with Jesus? Didn't he tell Jesus there was no one else they could turn to?

Yet here, at the end of Jesus' ministry, fear got the best of the otherwise faithful Peter. His reaction, after following Jesus for three years, perplexes us. Who wouldn't have known that he followed Jesus? After all, he had done it publicly, before all Israel. Denying it at the end seems a bit odd.

Yet this was only the start of Peter's painful reaction to fear—before the night was over, the disciple would deny the Master twice more.

We may not be able to explain Peter's reaction, but we certainly can understand the temptation that led him there. We too have faced disapproval and disastrous consequences as a result of our beliefs. Perhaps Peter even feared for his own life. *What will happen to me and the other disciples with the Master out of the way?* he may have asked himself.

We all have soft spots when it comes to temptation. In a flash, long periods of faithfulness can be threatened when Satan touches those places. Like Peter, we are human, but we too serve the risen Lord, who turns us to Himself again.

Impulsive Choice

"Look, I am about to die," Esau said. "What good is the birthright to me?" But Jacob said, "Swear to me first." So he swore an oath to him, selling his birthright to Jacob. Then Jacob gave Esau some bread and some lentil stew. He ate and drank, and then got up and left.

GENESIS 25:32–34 NIV

Was Esau really into drama, with this willingness to sell his birthright for bread and lentil stew out of fear that he would die? He certainly lacked judgment. That birthright was much more valuable than a single meal, even if it had been a four-star one with many courses.

Though it took time for Esau to realize what he'd given away, he did, and then he didn't blame himself but his brother.

Judgment is an important element of decision-making. A lot of things feed into our judgment: our past experiences with decision-making, our worldview, our education, and our faith. How we react shows much about where we have been, how we think, and what we've experienced.

Esau was rather impulsive. "I'll give anything up for food" isn't a well-thought-out decision. Maybe, as he traveled home, he had been thinking about how hungry he was, and smelling that delicious meal tempted him; but a less impulsive person would have immediately realized that what he was giving up was worth a much higher price.

Do we judge too quickly and later regret our choices? Then let's lift our concerns up to God, bring all our past learning to bear on a choice, and make a wise one.

Delay, Not Deny

*When Saul saw the vast Philistine army, he became frantic
with fear. He asked the LORD what he should do, but the LORD
refused to answer him. . . . Saul then said to his advisers,
"Find a woman who is a medium, so I can go and ask her what
to do." His advisers replied, "There is a medium at Endor."*

1 SAMUEL 28:5–7 NLT

Terror filled Saul's heart when he saw the Philistine army sitting on the tribe of Issachar's land. Saul knew that his enemy, David, was allied with the Philistines and might join them in battle against Israel. Who knew how many of his own men would flock to David's standard?

Saul was already cooking in this very hot pot when he discovered that when God said He had removed His anointing from him, it meant He would not answer prayers. The pressure turned up too high.

With Samuel dead and no one to turn to, the confused king went against his own command—and scripture's—and sought a medium. God had warned his people: "'Do not turn to mediums or seek out spiritists, for you will be defiled by them. I am the LORD your God'" (Leviticus 19:31 NIV), but Saul had slid far down the spiritual ladder by now. Even obvious faith issues were uncertain to him, and this choice reflected that change.

When God delays, He does not always deny—a lesson Saul never learned. Unlike Saul, when we're under pressure, let's await God's timing and continue to seek His face.

Spirit Living

When Simon saw that the Spirit was given at the laying on of the apostles'
hands, he offered them money and said, "Give me also this ability so
that everyone on whom I lay my hands may receive the Holy Spirit."
ACTS 8:18–19 NIV

For Simon, the whole world, even spiritual things, must have revolved around money. He saw the Spirit touching lives through the apostles' laying on of hands and thought it was some sort of magic he could make profit from.

Though he'd been baptized, it's hard to believe that Simon understood much about the commitment of living in the Spirit. Peter doesn't denounce Simon as an unbeliever, so perhaps he was simply still caught up in the trappings of his former sorcery, but the apostle set him apart from ministry until he'd dealt with his sin.

Very new Christians, especially those who have had little contact with the church, have little knowledge of the faith they've espoused. Jumping right into God's Word is their best choice so they can learn the way God wants His people to live and how to avoid "the sin that so easily entangles" (Hebrews 12:1 NIV).

For older Christians trapped in sin, making the choice to avoid sinful habits still comes hard. We all know the hurt that comes with shedding a "comfortable" sin. Only when God makes it more painful for us to stay in our wrongdoing may we be prompted to move away from it. But ultimately, any short-term pain invariably is less than the joy of living for Jesus.

Move Ahead in Confidence

Zelophehad. . .had five daughters. . . . One day his daughters went to the sacred tent. . . . The young women said: You know that our father died in the desert. . . . Our father left no sons to carry on his family name. But why should his name die out for that reason? Give us some land like the rest of his relatives in our clan, so our father's name can live on.

NUMBERS 27:1–4 CEV

Women inheriting land? That was pretty much unheard of in Zelophehad's day. But five daughters with no dowry would have been a real drain on the support network of Zelophehad's extended family, and these young women may have become rather independently minded because they grew up without brothers.

Their lack of brothers in a patriarchal society (in which men usually held land and had authority) was no one's fault. God simply hadn't given Zelophehad sons. But that didn't mean He didn't care about his daughters.

The culture they lived in didn't stop these courageous women. They went to Moses and asked if, when the land was divided, they might have their father's inheritance. They wanted to honor him by keeping the family alive.

As women, we should take Zelophehad's daughters' example to heart. Sometimes doing the right thing goes against our culture's trends or traditions. But that doesn't mean we should stop in our tracks. If our goal is within God's will, we can move ahead in confidence. When we want to do the right thing, we can know He will be right there with us.

Right There in Troubles

Moses and Aaron went to the king of Egypt and told him,
"The Lord God says, 'Let my people go into the desert,
so they can honor me with a celebration there.'"

EXODUS 5:1 CEV

*E*verything was against them, politically, when Moses and Aaron decided to obey God and confront the leader of one of the most powerful nations in the Middle East.

They had to know they weren't going to receive a warm welcome, but the brothers didn't let that set them back. God had given them a mission, and no one on earth would stop them.

It was a long, hard mission. No one, not even their own people, approved of the way they handled it, and the dangers were many, but they slogged on, when necessary. Discouragement could have turned them back, but they still kept repeating the command God gave in the beginning: "Let my people go."

You have to give them credit for their stubborn faithfulness. Through hordes of bugs, bloody water, and the rest of the disgusting methods God used to get through to Pharaoh, Moses and Aaron worked together as a team.

We tend to think "you can't fight city hall," and that it only gets harder to challenge authority at its highest levels. We easily give up on politicians who don't seem to have our best interests in mind. Maybe we need to take a lesson from these brothers who were determined to make God's command a reality, no matter what.

Remember, when faithfulness is hard, God will never let His people down. He's right there with them, no matter where they serve Him.

Second-Time Success

*Then the LORD said to Joshua, "Do not be afraid; do not
be discouraged. Take the whole army with you, and go up
and attack Ai. For I have delivered into your hands the king
of Ai, his people, his city and his land. You shall do to
Ai and its king as you did to Jericho and its king."*

JOSHUA 8:1–2 NIV

Wouldn't it be great if, at your most discouraging decision-
making moment, you knew that you couldn't lose? Joshua
got that reassurance from God after Israel had lost a battle at the
seemingly insignificant city of Ai, when "the Israelites were paralyzed
with fear at this turn of events, and their courage melted away"
(Joshua 7:5 NLT).

God dealt with the sin that caused the initial loss and told
Joshua, "Since the sin has been dealt with, attack again. The city
will fall into your hands." Joshua still made up a careful battle plan.
He wasn't leaving anything to chance.

This time, the city fell into Israel's hands with no trouble. But
it wasn't the battle plan or extra troops that made the difference:
it was God.

We usually don't get such a promise from God, but until we've
confessed our sin and taken action, we can't know if He'll smooth
the way for our most challenging choices. When we've lifted our
path up to God, asking for His guidance, and listened for His will,
the only option is to move ahead in faith.

Even when we've failed before, we can have secondary success if
we've made things right with Him.

A Repeated Challenge

David said, "You're a man, aren't you? And who is like you in Israel?
Why didn't you guard your lord the king? Someone came to destroy
your lord the king. What you have done is not good. As surely as the
LORD lives, you and your men must die, because you did not guard
your master, the LORD's anointed. Look around you. Where are the
king's spear and water jug that were near his head?"

1 SAMUEL 26:15–16 NIV

Twice, the outlaw David, who only deserted King Saul when
the king threatened to murder him, had the opportunity to
kill his enemy. Saul held the throne God had promised to David, and
striking his enemy first must have been a temptation. David's men
even encouraged him to murder Saul the first time Saul was near,
but the most David would do was cut a piece from the king's robe,
to prove how close he'd been (1 Samuel 24:4). Even that brought on
guilt later. David knew that God had anointed both kings and that
their lives were in His hands.

When a second opportunity to take Saul's life came, David
again proved how close he'd been to the king. This time, instead of
threatening the king's person, David proved Commander Abner's
lapse and blamed him for not being aware that his king's enemy
was at hand.

Though a bad choice was twice put before David, he steadfastly
continued to make the right one. Can we do the same when temptation repeatedly calls us to do wrong?

Exercise in Frustration

"How can I curse those whom God has not cursed?
How can I denounce those whom the LORD has not denounced?"
NUMBERS 23:8 NIV

God made it perfectly clear to the Mesopotamian prophet Balaam: Israel was His people, and they would overwhelm the Promised Land. Nothing King Balak of Moab could do would stop His purpose, and Balaam was not to serve him by cursing God's people.

One thing you can say about Balak: he was persistent. Again and again, he tempted the prophet to side with him against Israel. When Balaam first refused to come to him, the king sent for him again. God allowed the prophet to go, but the message never changed. To make certain Balaam got the picture, an angel of the Lord barred his way and Balaam's donkey spoke.

Again and again, Balaam repeated God's message to the frustrated king. Seven bulls sacrificed didn't change the message; moving the place of sacrifice had no effect; offers of great wealth did not change the prophet's consistency. Three times the prophet blessed the people Balak wanted cursed, though it angered the king.

God's will cannot be manipulated, and woe to the human who tries to do so. It will be an exercise in frustration for people today, just as it was for Balak.

Are we trying to manipulate God's will because our paths have been blocked? Better to reconsider and seek His direction instead.

Mixed Messages

～～～～～～～～～

*"[The Midianite women] were the ones who followed Balaam's
advice and enticed the Israelites to be unfaithful to the* LORD
in the Peor incident, so that a plague struck the LORD's *people."*
NUMBERS 31:16 NIV

❧

When we first meet Balaam in scripture, it seems as if he might actually have faith in the Lord. Over and over God tells the prophet not to curse His people, and Balaam stands firm against King Balak. We're tempted to believe this was an act of real faith.

But when we read the whole biblical record, something doesn't quite add up. Balaam engaged in divination, something God forbade (Numbers 24:1; Leviticus 19:26). And it seems unlikely that God would use a donkey as a messenger when He could just as well speak to Balaam directly. There just seems to be something a bit off with this prophet.

Despite God's clear message that His people were blessed, Balaam found a way to bring a curse down on the people of Israel, advising the Moabites to draw God's people away from Him through seduction. Their women drew Israel into sexual immorality, and what the Moabites started, the Midianites continued.

For his faithless act, the Word repeatedly denounces the inconsistent prophet (Deuteronomy 23:3–4; Revelation 2:14).

Today we'll run into people who give us mixed messages about their beliefs. Before we trust them and end up in a difficult situation, let's remember that the end of any story can be very different from the beginning. We don't need to judge others' faith, but we can be careful about letting them lead us astray.

Redeeming Bad Choices

But when [the elders of Israel] said, "Give us a king to lead us,"
this displeased Samuel; so he prayed to the LORD. And the LORD
told him: "Listen to all that the people are saying to you; it is not
you they have rejected, but they have rejected me as their king."

1 SAMUEL 8:6–7 NIV

*F*eeling rejected, Samuel brought his troubles to the Lord. Though the prophet had obeyed God's command and warned His people of the heavy price they'd pay for having a king (1 Samuel 8:10–18), the rebellious Israelites refused to accept God alone as their ruler. God put His finger on the prophet's worst hurts when he replied that it was not Samuel who was rejected but Himself.

God didn't complain, but knowing His love portrayed in scripture, He almost certainly felt the pain of rejection. Foreseeing the troubles Saul would cause His people and the warfare that would result from Saul's failures and David's anointing as king, God must have grieved over their choice; yet He let it stand.

Israel paid the price Samuel foretold, but God eventually used this rejection as an opportunity to put the man after His own heart into power (Acts 13:22), the forefather of His Son, the Messiah.

As with Israel, God can bring good things out of our mistakes, but often at a high price. Though God can redeem even our bad choices and use them to His purpose, how much better it is if we never experience the pain of having rejected our Lord.

The Best Choice

*In heaven I have only you, and on this earth you
are all I want. My body and mind may fail,
but you are my strength and my choice forever.*
PSALM 73:25–26 CEV

One choice forms the basis for all our lives: our best choice, the one upon which all others hang, is our relationship with God.

Do we believe we can avoid making a choice? Then we're fooling ourselves. We can decide to trust in God or not trust in Him, but there is no state of neutrality. None of us can be the Switzerland of faith because God doesn't give us that option. We are for Him or against Him, but we can't just tepidly like Him. We either love God or we don't. A neutral heart cannot serve.

Devoting ourselves to our Lord means we choose to go whole-heartedly for Him. We cast our lot in with Him and leave behind whatever is not of Him, because no half-hearted devotion brings us into eternity with Jesus.

When we cast ourselves upon Jesus, He becomes the only thing we want in life, the only choice that matters. Whether we are healthy or ill, whether our minds are sharp or dulled by age, He is our permanent choice, the One we cling to persistently. Faith in God is a lifelong choice, one we should never dare to back out on.

Better Choice?

If I live, it will be for Christ, and if I die, I will gain even more. . . . It is a hard choice to make. I want to die and be with Christ, because that would be much better.

PHILIPPIANS 1:21, 23 CEV

In rough times, Christians are often drawn heavenward. *How wonderful it would be,* we think, *to end this life and live in eternal bliss.* God placed heaven in our hearts as He brought us to salvation, and we feel the pull of eternity.

But heaven is not the only goal God has for our lives. He placed us on earth for a purpose, though our vision of it may grow rather dim at times. When life becomes difficult, we may toy with the idea of how wonderful it will be to slip from our mortal bodies. But let's remember that selfish desire sets aside both the joys of this earth that are yet to come and the good God has prepared for us to do here.

Paul knew the desire for heaven and longed to be with Jesus for eternity, but he also recognized that the churches he ministered to had great need of him. Certainly the congregations in Greece and Asia Minor did not want to lose him and discouraged him from heading to dangerous Jerusalem.

Yet God had a greater ministry for Paul in Rome when He sent him to prison there. Bars, rock walls, and suffering could not stop the Gospel.

Living for Christ may be hard, but what good things might the Lord bring from the struggles we face?

God, Our Help

Let all who are helpless, listen and be glad. . . . I asked the
LORD for help, and he saved me from all my fears.
PSALM 34:2, 4 CEV

Sometimes, as we face a serious decision, helplessness may overwhelm us. Why did God trust us with such a large or scary decision that risks our lives or our futures?

David wrote these words after he'd been in a very dangerous situation. Again, Saul had tried to kill David, who fled to Gath. But Achish, the king (or Abimelech) of Gath knew and feared David's reputation for killing ten thousands. Perceiving the danger he was in, David needed a quick way out, so he pretended to be mad. The king couldn't have the threatening soldier leave soon enough.

Fear was not an emotion David was a stranger to. He'd faced death on the battlefield and nearly been skewered by Saul's spear. More than that, he knew that others too were prone to fearfulness. So he penned this testimony to God's faithfulness.

Let those who are afflicted with helplessness hear the psalmist's cry. When times were very hard for David, he called out to God, and the Faithful One not only protected David's life, but He also saved him from the fears that could have incapacitated him. Later, he added: "Come to him for protection, and you will be glad" (v. 8 CEV).

Are you feeling helpless? Turn to God, who is your help. He will never let you down.

Christ Focused

Let the message about Christ completely fill your lives, while
you use all your wisdom to teach and instruct each other. With
thankful hearts, sing psalms, hymns, and spiritual songs to God.
Whatever you say or do should be done in the name of the
Lord Jesus, as you give thanks to God the Father because of him.
COLOSSIANS 3:16–17 CEV

*D*o you want to be a wholehearted Christian? In just a couple of verses, Paul succinctly describes the kind of congregation that will encourage you to grow in Jesus. Faithful interaction with those who know and love God and want others to share that blessing encourages believers in their faith.

Are you seeking a church? Keep these things in mind. Find a congregation where members support one another instead of engaging in criticism and backbiting. Worship and thankfulness are the hallmarks of God's people. Their faithfulness to scripture and their attention to instruction in the Word should form the base of all their actions.

Choosing a church is an important decision in your life. Whether you are young, single, and need the support of others who do not have a nearby family or you have young children who need a good youth program, or whether you are an older couple or a mature single, do not sell yourself short by becoming involved in a church that has not made Christ its focus.

Through fellowship with others who have God at the center of their church life, you will become a strong believer.

Things That Really Matter

*You have a choice—do you want the L*ORD *to bless you,*
or do you want him to put a curse on you? Today I am
giving you his laws, and if you obey him, he will bless you.
But if you disobey him and worship those gods that have
*never done anything for you, the L*ORD *will put a curse on you.*
DEUTERONOMY 11:26–28 CEV

Every morning, we face a whole day of choices, large and small. Some, like whether we have coffee or tea for breakfast, are fairly minor. We easily make such decisions, based on our whims of the moment. We're unlikely to have any earth-shattering changes in our lives because we choose one kind of beverage over another.

But we forever have the ability to make one choice that can permanently affect our lives: Will we obey God today? Tomorrow? Next week? We can make a decision to accept God one day, and it can touch our lives permanently, but the effect of that decision can be diminished if we do not continue choosing to follow in God's way on a daily basis. Those who think choosing God is a one-time deal that never requires follow-through are seriously mistaken.

Choices have consequences, and the ones we dedicate ourselves to will have the greatest impact on our lives. Commit to the things that really matter, follow through on them, and you'll be heading in the right direction.

Advice and Correction

*Pay attention to advice and accept
correction, so you can live sensibly.*
PROVERBS 19:20 CEV

"I did it my way" is never biblical advice. God understands the
importance of learning from those who have His wisdom and
encourages us to learn from others.

Of course, not all Christians have good advice to offer. You've
probably known some people who love God but whose example
would lead to disaster. Still, God has placed people in your life who
have wisdom that can lead to sensible decisions.

Looking for an adviser? Seek out someone who has the credentials.
Just as you'd want to hire a carpenter who knows how to use his
tools well, you'll want an adviser who knows how to use the Word
wisely to help you follow in God's ways. You're unlikely to want
advice from a Christian who has only known Jesus for a few weeks,
but a mature believer may set you on just the right path.

When we ask for advice, we open our lives to another. If the
advice is accompanied by some additional points of correction in
unexpected places, we need not take offense. Perhaps God is retuning
our lives through others. If we refuse to allow fellow believers to
take a wider view of our lives, we may miss out on the best God
has to offer.

Don't ignore advice, and don't refuse correction. They may be
the best things God wants to bring into your life.

Correct the World?

*The next morning some Jews formed a conspiracy
and bound themselves with an oath not to eat
or drink until they had killed Paul.*

ACTS 23:12 NIV

*D*id these men who opposed Paul after he appeared before the Sanhedrin carry through on their oath? Was it so important to them that Paul should die that they gave their own lives when they failed to take his? Somehow it seems unlikely that they starved themselves to death or suffered dehydration when Rome took over the apostle's case.

Did they fear the Lord enough that they paid with their lives? Or did they suddenly change their attitude about their oath, believing that putting Paul into Roman hands was enough?

In binding themselves to this oath, the conspirators missed out on one truth that should have been glaringly clear: promising to kill someone because you disagree with his beliefs is not a command of scripture. Perhaps in their own self-righteousness, they came to believe they had this right. Little did they know how wrong they were.

We may not aim to murder, but sometimes we are tempted to believe our ways are right while another's are wrong. Do we take off in our own self-righteousness or truly seek God's face about the issue? Are we open to correction or ready to correct the world on what's right and wrong?

Would we be willing to give our lives for that opinion or stand before God concerning its truth?

More Danger?

*Some time later Samson fell in love with a woman
named Delilah, who lived in the valley of Sorek.*
JUDGES 16:4 NLT

When it came to women, Samson just didn't seem to get it. The more seductive they appeared, the better this Israelite judge liked them. It didn't matter that they didn't share his faith or couldn't easily be part of the Jewish community; Samson liked them exotic and dangerous.

This wasn't the first time Samson had become involved with a woman who was from his enemies' camp. He had married another Philistine woman, and though God used the unwise marital choice to work against the Philistines, the relationship turned into a personal disaster for the judge.

Unfazed, Samson didn't learn from his first mistake. He went and fell for a Philistine woman all over again, with even more disastrous results. Delilah had *dysfunction* written all over her, but Samson couldn't see that. He ran right down the same road he'd followed before and got himself into even more danger.

Are we learning from the mistakes we've made in past decisions? We may make better choices than Samson concerning our romantic involvements, but perhaps in other areas we have been less successful than this judge.

It's understandable that we all will make mistakes, but are certain patterns of poor decision-making showing up frequently in our lives? If so, let's consistently bring those weaknesses to God in prayer, painful as it may be to admit our errors. He can help us find better choices and put them to work in our lives.

Ark Building

"So make yourself an ark of cypress wood; make rooms
in it and coat it with pitch inside and out."

GENESIS 6:14 NIV

God came to Noah and commanded him to build an ark.
Noah must have had a lot of questions: "An ark, Lord? What's
an ark?" Or, "What's going on, Lord?" So God gave him lots of answers.

God had never done such a thing before, and His whole plan
defied Noah's understanding. But Noah still trusted his Lord. He
spent hours building a boat he'd never seen the likes of before. He
coated it with pitch (which must have been a nasty job) then waited
for God to complete the next part of His plan.

All that time, Noah must have had questions about God's goal.
Perhaps the idea that God would destroy all living things outside the ark made him nervous. He had to wonder how this would
end. But God had commanded, and Noah obeyed, despite his
questions.

More than once in our lives we land in situations like Noah's.
God may not share as many details of His plan with us as He did
with Noah, but we are sure He has moved in our lives. We follow,
perhaps confused a bit but faithful.

God doesn't have to give us His whole plan. But He makes it clear
that we need to obey.

Is there an ark you need to start building today?

Who Goes Before Us?

"Go up to the land flowing with milk and honey. But I will not go with you, because you are a stiff-necked people and I might destroy you on the way. . . ." Then Moses said to him, "If your Presence does not go with us, do not send us up from here. How will anyone know that you are pleased with me and with your people unless you go with us? What else will distinguish me and your people from all the other people on the face of the earth?"

EXODUS 33:3, 15–16 NIV

How angry God must have been with His people to send them into the Promised Land on their own—at least, that's what it sounded like to Moses, who expected to be at the head of this huge band of invaders. Moses didn't want to go anywhere without God because he knew this would be a dangerous mission and didn't want to set out on his own.

When we set out on a project for God, whether it's teaching a Sunday school class, taking part in a church ministry, or simply loving our families for God, do we look to see that God is going before us? Or do we choose to set out on our own?

When God leads the way, we are known as His people, under His care. Though going it alone can make the journey tough, walking in His footsteps brings us to just the right place at the right time.

Isn't that where we want to be?

Prodigal Son

*"Not long after that, the younger son got together
all he had, set off for a distant country and
there squandered his wealth in wild living."*
LUKE 15:13 NIV

The Prodigal Son is a sterling example of bad decision-making. He couldn't wait to get his money before he ran off to a strange land to spend it. Finally, destitute, he landed in a field, tending pigs.

We tend to look at the son and feel some pride. We've never done such a thing, have we? We ask ourselves how he could have been so foolish, and we feel good about ourselves. But in doing so, we miss the point of Jesus' parable. We are all prodigals who ran from God; none of us made a good choice until we turned to follow Him. The Prodigal Son, who runs back to his father when he's in trouble, is actually a good example because he does that. But we often forget about this son's good choice, a choice we need to share.

When we make bad choices, are we ready to turn to the Father who loves us? Or will we so fear Him that we avoid His face? Can we turn to Him, asking forgiveness?

Be assured that your Father loves you and is calling you home. No mistake or sin of yours can stop His love, and He'll be ready to throw a party as soon as He sees you in the distance.

First Step

The LORD *had said to Abram, "Leave your native country, your*
relatives, and your father's family, and go to the land that I will
show you. I will make you into a great nation. I will bless you
and make you famous, and you will be a blessing to others."
GENESIS 12:1–2 NLT

*M*ove, Abram; go to a perfectly strange place where you don't
know the neighbors and don't even know if they'll be nice
to you. Without a home to buy or a friend to show you where the
best neighborhood is, set out to this place you've never even seen."
God asked much of Abram when He told him to move. The promises
were many, but Abram's future must have seemed rather ethereal.

Abram had both feet planted firmly in midair when he chose to
follow God's command. All he knew was that God wanted him to
go and promised to bless him for his obedience.

We can relate to that, can't we? The Word tells us of the many
blessings that come from obedience, but the way can be hard. Our
pilgrimage of faith leaves us with many questions about the natives
we'll encounter in our new land, the way we must travel to get there,
and the benefits that will be ours when we follow God.

Like Abram, when we leave the land of unbelief and push off into
faith, we step out into the air. Our trust is in the One who calls us.

Though the way is long and hard, we will never be sorry we took
that first step.

Both Hands

*"Sir, do you remember me?" Hannah asked. "I am the very woman
who stood here several years ago praying to the LORD. I asked
the LORD to give me this boy, and he has granted my request.
Now I am giving him to the LORD, and he will belong to the
LORD his whole life." And they worshiped the LORD there.*
1 SAMUEL 1:26–28 NLT

Hannah most wanted a son—someone to relieve the disgrace of barrenness and to care for her in her old age. She prayed fiercely to have that boy, and God sent him. But Samuel came at a price: Hannah had to decide to give him up to God.

When Hannah promised that in prayer, she meant her words, and though it might have been a struggle, she did not fail God. Hannah gifted Samuel back to the Lord, and she gave him completely. Instead of having him taught about God locally, she gave him to Eli, the priest in charge of the sanctuary that held the Ark of the Covenant. She saw Samuel only once a year.

It was a good opportunity for her son, but how she must have missed him. The honor of having a child being raised to serve the Lord probably didn't fully kill the pain of that loss.

When we give anything up to God, will we do so completely? Or will we hold on to it with one hand? Only gifts given with both hands are fully given.

Second Chances

Then Peter, filled with the Holy Spirit, said to them: "Rulers and elders of the people! If we are being called to account today for an act of kindness shown to a man who was lame and are being asked how he was healed, then know this, you and all the people of Israel: It is by the name of Jesus Christ of Nazareth, whom you crucified but whom God raised from the dead, that this man stands before you healed."

ACTS 4:8–10 NIV

Objections to the healing of a lame man? It's hard to imagine that anyone would have them, especially in an age when medicine was so limited. But Peter and John were brought before the Sanhedrin because of it.

It wasn't really that the elders of Israel objected to someone being well, but they were concerned about losing their spiritual grip on the nation. Others could see as clearly as they that the apostles had a special power at work in them.

Peter, the man who had denied Christ, allowed the Spirit to control him, and this outcome was very different from his earlier failures. Instead of hiding from the people who had spiritual power over Israel, he spoke out clearly and with conviction, testifying to the power of Jesus. He who had denied his Lord had come full circle in faith.

Do you have a spiritual failure in your past? Don't let it stop you in your tracks. God's power is still at work in you, if you choose to let Him have sway over your spirit, thoughts, and actions.

The Lord of second chances has one for you.

In God's Toolbox

When the messengers returned, they told Jacob, "We went to your brother Esau, and now he is heading this way with four hundred men." Jacob was so frightened that he divided his people, sheep, cattle, and camels into two groups. He thought, "If Esau attacks one group, perhaps the other can escape."
GENESIS 32:6–8 CEV

There's nothing like fear to clarify our thinking processes—or turn them all to mush.

When Jacob heard that the brother he'd wronged was on his way with four hundred men, the consequences of his actions became perfectly clear. So did the danger in which he'd placed himself and all his family. Jacob took action.

But so did God. Responding to Jacob's immediate, fervent prayer for protection, He worked in both men's hearts. So Jacob sent conciliatory gifts to his wronged brother, and Esau forgave the brother who had stolen his birthright.

The fears that threatened to turn Jacob's brain to mush actually worked to his benefit as they changed his heart toward his own sin and the brother he'd wronged. Instead of flailing about in a frenzy, Jacob admitted his sin and sought forgiveness.

God doesn't want us to live in fear, but sometimes, as with Jacob, He'll use fear to make us realize and accept our own failures. When terror becomes a wake-up call, it can be a good thing in our lives. As it causes us to turn to our Lord and make better choices, it's a valuable gadget in God's toolbox.

More Security

*But a Samaritan, as he traveled, came where the man was;
and when he saw him, he took pity on him. He went to
him and bandaged his wounds, pouring on oil and wine.
Then he put the man on his own donkey, brought
him to an inn and took care of him.*

LUKE 10:33–34 NIV

Why should the Samaritan have come to the rescue of the robbed man? When a priest and Levite had already bypassed the victim, fearing that they might be compromised or similarly attacked, why should a foreigner take on the task?

Though other Jews bypassed the man, the despised outsider treated the man's wounds, placed him gently on his own donkey, and stopped at an inn along the way. There he paid for the man's needs and promised more money for his entire stay. If there was a Good Samaritan in real life, he was certainly a stunningly openhearted man.

God calls us to be the Good Samaritans in our world. Instead of merely looking out for our own welfare, He wants us to choose generosity and selflessness. That goes against the grain of all our world teaches us; even the priest and Levite, religious men, followed the world's advice, kept themselves safe, and ignored the love God calls us to.

Generosity and selflessness or safety? Which will we choose? Which holds more security—God or the world?

Seeds of Dissension

And Jonadab, the son of Shimeah David's brother,
answered and said, Let not my lord suppose that they
have slain all the young men the king's sons; for Amnon
only is dead: for by the appointment of Absalom this hath
been determined from the day that he forced his sister Tamar.
2 SAMUEL 13:32 KJV

It's hard to know what to think of Absalom. He was a brother who wanted to see justice done to the man who had raped his sister; and his father, King David, seemed unlikely, even after a long time, to give that justice. But we can hardly agree with the murder Absalom committed when he took justice into his own hands. While we feel sorry for the king's son, we can't agree with his solution to the problem.

But the poor choices that led to murder didn't start with Absalom. As king, David should have commanded justice for his daughter. Scripture never tells us why he failed to do so, but it shows us the result of failed justice against a perpetrator of a most intimate act of sin. When David averted his eyes to the wrong, it wreaked havoc in his own intimate life, destroying part of his family.

We also need to be aware of justice in our personal lives. Do we treat family members well, as equals, or do we choose to play favorites and sow the seeds of dissension?

Where justice rules, so does peace.

Indulgent Sin

*I meant that you are not to associate with anyone who claims
to be a believer yet indulges in sexual sin, or is greedy,
or worships idols, or is abusive, or is a drunkard,
or cheats people. Don't even eat with such people.*

1 CORINTHIANS 5:11 NLT

Our world is far from perfect, and it doesn't take long to run into people who have done the things Paul warned against in his letter to the Corinthians. How can we respond?

First, let's be clear on one thing: this verse isn't talking about separating ourselves from everyone who's ever strayed from righteous living. To do so, we might have to remove ourselves to some far peak and avoid most human contact. This verse *is* telling us to avoid Christians who regularly indulge in sin. Believers who are unfaithful to their spouses, greedy, or regularly fall into other spiritual failures are hypocrites, and God doesn't want us communing with them.

We may like such sinners. They may have plenty of charm—and that's the problem. A charmless sinner would be unlikely to lead us astray, but appealing ones are likely to stay in our lives and slowly make wrongdoing look enjoyable. God doesn't want us inviting such temptation into our lives.

Deciding to avoid habitual sinners can be uncomfortable. Perhaps we'll need to explain to others why we've made that choice or just quietly slip out of a circle of friends. But ignoring the apostle's warning could be even more uncomfortable if it leads us into indulgent sin that damages our relationships and love for God.

Deep Love

Most important of all, continue to show deep love for each other, for love covers a multitude of sins.
1 PETER 4:8 NLT

"Love is a choice." If you've been in Christian circles for long, you've heard this statement often.

Usually when we think about that phrase, we're considering how much love we have to expend on others who irritate us or want us to do things in a way that we don't appreciate.

But what about the multitude of sins we commit, perhaps without realizing it? How many people have opted to show us deep love by holding back a critical word, doing something for us when we didn't deserve it, or encouraging us when we felt down and became rather cranky. These may not have seemed like big sins from our side, but they still caused others to use restraint.

Many people have chosen to love us, even when we were less than lovely. They made that decision and probably brought a blessing into our lives. At the very least, they refrained from irritating us when we had a lot on our plates.

Today, be thankful for the people who have shown you deep love and covered over your sins, both large and small. You may not be able to repay their kind acts, but you can pass them on. The next time a child seems ready to test your last nerve, a coworker throws an unwanted project on your desk, or your best friend stands you up for a date, remember to show deep love.

Then sins will stop multiplying, and God will work in both your lives.

Desire

And he answering said, Thou shalt love the Lord thy God with all thy heart, and with all thy soul, and with all thy strength, and with all thy mind; and thy neighbour as thyself. And he said unto him, Thou hast answered right: this do, and thou shalt live. But he, willing to justify himself, said unto Jesus, And who is my neighbour?

LUKE 10:27–29 KJV

This lawyer knew his law book—the Word of God. As soon as Jesus asked him what the law said, he snapped back with this canned reply.

The problem wasn't one of understanding; it was one of desire. The legal beagle knew what God commanded—he just didn't want to do it.

We've found ourselves in the same dilemma. We understand what God calls us to do, but we balk at doing it. Maybe it isn't convenient. Or we fear the pain that comes with spiritual discipline. Our failing hearts may even want, in some deep corner, to obey God, but it just seems too hard.

The answer to this faith conundrum is that obedience *is* too hard. Under our own power, we will never obey God. If we determined to do everything God wanted us to do, even with the best will in the world, it would remain an impossible goal.

God isn't looking for perfection from us—He knows we could never achieve that. But He is looking for a desire to obey. If we want to be willing to do His will, His Spirit can begin to work in our lives.

So what do we desire?

No Faith for Sissies!

But I say unto you, Love your enemies, bless them that curse
you, do good to them that hate you, and pray for them
which despitefully use you, and persecute you.

MATTHEW 5:44 KJV

Christianity is no faith for sissies! Forgiving those who hurt us
and even persecute us is hard work, because when God tells
us to do these things, He isn't simply expecting lip service. Our
hearts have to be changed to love enemies, bless cursers, do good
to haters, and pray for those who mistreat and persecute us. God
isn't talking about quick, hypocritical "bless that so-and-so" prayers.

Getting to the point where we can pray honestly for enemies
isn't just an emotional experience that helps us love them—though
emotions may play a part in it. We have to decide to obey God, though
it takes every fiber of our wills to do so. Even then, we can't begin
to put that decision into action without God's Spirit working in us.

God often brings one of His truths to us, asking for our obedience,
and leaves the decision to us. Once we know His will, we should
obey; but how hard that can be! Loving enemies takes a lot of
spiritual strength.

However, once we commit to obedience, His Spirit can flood our
lives, helping us act on that decision. The choice we thought was so
hard becomes a blessed opportunity.

Will we choose His way or our own? Obedience or willfulness?
Or are we sissies?

Positive Impact

*Wherefore, my beloved brethren, let every man
be swift to hear, slow to speak, slow to wrath.*
JAMES 1:19 KJV

Our mouths can get us into so much trouble because our natural tendency seems to be to open them before our brains engage. Even when we don't mean to do damage, we can hurt others with careless words.

The apostle James knew how difficult the tongue could be and warned us about it in the third chapter of his epistle, concluding, "With the tongue we praise our Lord and Father, and with it we curse human beings, who have been made in God's likeness" (3:9 NIV).

Like us, James had probably heard enough church gossip to turn his stomach. He'd talked to people who were hurt by words spoken by fellow Christians, and he knew that harsh words wound more deeply when they come from a sibling in Christ. Therefore, the apostle warned the brethren to have good listening skills, thoughtful speech, and restrained anger. He knew that this pattern of interaction with other Christians would bring a great harvest of kindness in the church, which could overflow into the world and rub off on unbelievers.

Like those first-century Christians, we need to think before we speak, control our anger, and decide to speak words that build up, gently redirect, and encourage others. How we choose to say things can be as important as the message we want to share. When we speak kindly, our words can have a positive impact beyond anything we expected.

Taking Credit

As he was about to enter Egypt, [Abram] said to his wife Sarai,
"I know what a beautiful woman you are. When the Egyptians
see you, they will say, 'This is his wife.' Then they will kill me but
will let you live. Say you are my sister, so that I will be treated
well for your sake and my life will be spared because of you."
GENESIS 12:11–13 NIV

No question about it, Abram's life could have been in danger. Here he was, a stranger with a beautiful wife and many possessions. Who would miss him in Egypt if he suddenly disappeared? What an easy way for another man to gain his wife and goods.

Abram may not have been thinking of royalty when he asked his wife to tell that little white lie. After all, the couple may have excused themselves, she *was* his sister—they simply wouldn't be telling about their more intimate relationship. But when Pharaoh took Sarai into his harem, the couple landed in real trouble. As she headed for the palace, Sarai must have wondered what would have happened had she told the truth, and perhaps she blamed Abram for their troubles.

When we make decisions based on another's advice, let's remember that *we* made those choices, however bad they were, and we are responsible for them. Others' input cannot relieve us from the burden of a wrong choice, and throwing blame on another never solves a problem.

We make the choice, and we must take credit for the results, whatever they are.

Who's on First?

Jesus answered, "If you want to be perfect, go, sell your possessions
and give to the poor, and you will have treasure in heaven.
Then come, follow me." When the young man heard this,
he went away sad, because he had great wealth.

MATTHEW 19:21–22 NIV

The rich young ruler had everything this world could offer physically. But it still wasn't enough. Empty inside, he came to Jesus, his desolation showing through his questions and attitudes. Every effort to obey the law, though it may not have been as perfect as he indicated to Jesus, had brought him to a place in his life God had intended: he was aware of his own inability to gain the spiritually full life he desired.

The rich young man attracted Jesus, and Jesus attracted him too. Certainly he'd come to the right place to find answers, but the prominent man walked away saddened because the price was too great.

Though he didn't know it, the ruler had a God-shaped space in his heart that only Jesus could fill. None of those earthly delights could sate his desire. We'd like to hope that his spiritual emptiness constantly drew him back to Jesus and that he eventually committed to Him, but scripture doesn't tell us so.

We all find ourselves in the rich young ruler's place at least once in our lives. Will we put Jesus first in our lives or fall prey to the things of the world?

Who's on first in your life?

Do unto Others

"Do not judge, or you too will be judged. For in the same way you judge others, you will be judged, and with the measure you use, it will be measured to you."
MATTHEW 7:1–2 NIV

Many non-Christians have used the first of these verses to condemn believers for telling them their lifestyles are not pleasing to God. That has stopped plenty of Christian mouths. But reading only the first sentence in Jesus' story can give people the wrong impression of what He was really saying.

That sentence was intended as an attention-getter for the people listening to His story, not as a final takeaway. And the second verse makes it clear that Jesus is talking about compassion, not a complete inability to judge.

Whether or not those critics realize it, we all make judgments daily about people and their actions. And while some believers may be harsh in their opinions of those who do not share their faith, non-Christians can judge just as harshly. All of us, saint and sinner, have a critical side that may come out when people disagree with us. Just see how "open-minded" some non-Christians are when Christians give their opinions in public.

Judgment decisions need to be made carefully and gently. That's what these verses are all about. If we don't want to be treated to rough criticism, we shouldn't hand it out to others, because we will open ourselves up to retaliation and will not lead others to Christ.

"Do to others," when you need to judge, "as you would have them do to you" (Luke 6:31 NIV).

Life Sacrifice

To do what is right and just is more acceptable
to the Lord than sacrifice.

PROVERBS 21:3 NIV

All the animal sacrifices the Jews could offer up meant nothing if their hearts were in the wrong place, because clean hearts and sacrifice are inexorably connected. No animal sacrifice could make a sinful heart clean; all the blood of bulls and doves cannot change a heart that rebels against God.

Coming to the temple and paying for sacrifices didn't mean the Jews were doing more than plunking down hard cash in exchange for an animal's life. Religious rites don't equate to faith because a perfectly heartless person can engage in them without caring a bit about God. Many people have done "religious" things to look good to others, but they have had little to do with the state of their hearts.

But when we live our whole lives—not just a few days of them—doing right and seeing that justice is done, people begin to take notice. The pattern of our lives shows that we are willing to give up good things for the right and just ones, and even unbelievers begin to appreciate that kind of sacrifice.

We need to ask ourselves what our "right and just" quotient is. Is it a lifestyle or an occasional event? Do we daily seek to follow the Word or simply do it when it's convenient?

A life sacrifice is what God's really seeking. Are we willing to go that far?

Peaceful Living

Do your best to live at peace with everyone.
ROMANS 12:18 CEV

Living peacefully is a choice—one we sometimes cannot manage if the other party is unwilling to bury the hatchet. That's why God only commands us to do our best to live peacefully. But often, since "a soft answer turneth away wrath" (Proverbs 15:1 KJV), a lack of confrontation can bring a surprising amount of peace to relationships.

As we look at our warlike world, living at peace may seem impossible. And, left to human minds and hearts, it would be. People tend to jump into action against enemies, pushing weapons in their faces. But with God and decisions that reflect His will, we can begin to find peace with some. Where we cannot find peace, at least we can limit our own sinful actions and know that we have made our best efforts to obey Paul's counsel.

Contentious coworkers, neighbors, and even friends may never leave our lives entirely, but by living by biblical guidelines, we can deal with them more effectively. And when our abilities fail, God can still work wonderfully in our lives and in those of our neighbors.

The neighbor across the way may still aim his snow blower at the end of your driveway, but the town's plow will still carry it away. Your nerves may strain when a coworker takes advantage of you yet again, but God will help you keep your cool.

There is always a way to try to live at peace, and that's all God asks of you.

Love That Flows

But I am giving you a new command.
You must love each other, just as I have loved you.
JOHN 13:34 CEV

ohn 13:34 is one of those good news/bad news verses. It's great to love someone who fits into your life easily and shares many of your interests, attitudes, and beliefs; someone who is easygoing and considerate is a simple job to love, and you delight in obeying the command.

But how about the folks you don't see eye to eye with: the person in your church who always wants to pick a fight over the smallest thing, the coworker who expects you to be exacting on everything but isn't herself, the neighbor who plays loud music when you're trying to sleep, the person who hates Christians?

Each of us has a list of irritants that could fill a roll of cash-register tape.

God didn't tell us to love only the easy folks, and He didn't leave a loophole. "You *must* love each other" (emphasis added) doesn't allow us leeway to pick and choose. There isn't a person on earth, even an enemy, that Christians have a right to hate—even the ones on our long lists.

If Jesus could love His enemies enough to come and die for us, we can choose to follow in His footsteps. Though it strains our souls to the utmost, His Spirit fills our souls. In His power, love can flow into our world.

The Battle Is God's

Some people came and told Jehoshaphat, "A vast army is coming
against you from Edom, from the other side of the Dead Sea. . . ."
Alarmed, Jehoshaphat resolved to inquire of the Lord,
and he proclaimed a fast for all Judah. The people of Judah
came together to seek help from the Lord; indeed,
they came from every town in Judah to seek him.
2 Chronicles 20:2–4 NIV

Armies from neighboring countries had invaded Judah, and those surrounding nations had a vested interest in taking over the small country. There were no missiles to deter them, just valorous soldiers who would be greatly outnumbered.

When the nation looked to their king, peaceful Jehoshaphat unveiled an unusual battle plan. He brought all the people to the temple to beseech God to act for His people. Some might have thought he would have better spent his time preparing the army. But they would have been wrong.

It might have been an act of desperation, but Jehoshaphat's choice was the wise one. God's Spirit came upon Jahaziel, who told the people not to fear and gave Judah a battle plan: the battle was God's, not theirs. When the army went to the gorge God designated, they saw His amazing protection of them. Suddenly all the enemy troops began fighting among themselves. It became unnecessary for Israel to become involved.

Sometimes we need God to go before us and fight battles for which we have no strength. Will we let Him take the lead while we follow in faith? Do we understand that the battle is not ours alone?

Long-Term View

~~~~~~~~~~~~~~~~~~~~~~~~~~

[Potiphar's wife] kept begging Joseph day after day,
but he refused to do what she wanted or even to go near her.
GENESIS 39:10 CEV

ecoming sexually involved with his master's wife would have
been so easy for Joseph. She kept propositioning him and even
accused him of rape when he refused her one time too many. But
Joseph didn't follow soap-opera morality—he held up against the
pressure and consistently lived out his faith.

In putting his libido on hold, Joseph kept a long-term view in
mind. Valuing his master's good opinion and the commandments of
God, he held firm in the face of temptation. Though his unpopular
decision led him into great trouble, Joseph rested in the truth that
he had done right—the thing God could reward him for. Blessing
was long in coming, but it was as certain as the judgment that must
have fallen on Potiphar's wife. Joseph never retaliated, knowing he
could count on God for justice.

We too may have to stand firmly on right choices that honor
God. Though life seems to turn against us for a time and we suffer
for our obedience to our Lord, we can be certain God will bring us
through, just as He brought Joseph into a better place.

Today, do you need to take a long-term view that will see you
through?

A Way Back Home

If my own people will humbly pray and turn back to me
and stop sinning, then I will answer them from heaven.
I will forgive them and make their land fertile once again.
2 CHRONICLES 7:14 CEV

Have you had to make a strong decision to turn away from sin? It probably wasn't one of your life's best feel-good moments because sin is so comfortable and hard to shake off. According to the writer of Hebrews, sin easily besets us (12:1).

The Bible gives us many examples of those beset by sin: Cain, Samson, and Judas, just to name a few. Their stories don't end happily. But many others fought to overcome their transgressions and found themselves in a much better place: David and Peter, for example, fell but turned again toward God's grace. In that turning, their lives found redemption.

God made the promise of 2 Chronicles 7:14 as Solomon worshipped before the newly consecrated temple. Knowing His people would not remain constant forever, during this spiritual high, He gave them a way back to Himself.

Always there is a way back to God when we confess our sins and humble ourselves to do His will. At first our rebellious hearts may resist, but as we turn back home, to the Lord who loves us best, the joys of His love surround us. Our difficult decision past, we experience the great blessings that lie within His hand.

Overtaken?

"That is why I tell you not to worry about everyday life—whether you have enough food and drink, or enough clothes to wear. Isn't life more than food, and your body more than clothing?"

MATTHEW 6:25 NLT

Worry short-circuits decision-making; while our minds are in turmoil with fear for the future or past mistakes, we cannot think clearly. Our choices, clouded by our own lack of vision, run us into a fog-covered wall.

That's why Jesus tells us not to worry about our sustenance or clothes. "Look at the birds," He continued comfortingly. "They don't plant or harvest or store food in barns, for your heavenly Father feeds them. And aren't you far more valuable to him than they are?" (Matthew 6:26 NLT).

When troubles stare us in the face, it's hard to grab on to God and trust. But as His children, we have that right. Just as a toddler trustingly grasps his father's fingers, we can grab our Father's hand. Children never doubt their dad's comfort or dependability; he has never failed. How much more true that is of our heavenly Father, who is perfect and powerful.

Finally, Jesus asks, "Can all your worries add a single moment to your life?" (Matthew 6:27 NLT). What is the sense in worry? It traps our minds and hearts and offers no benefits. So why should we allow it to overtake us?

Overtaken by anxiety? Push it from your mind whenever it starts. Before it gets a grip on you, turn again to the Word and know that your Father loves you.

Hearts and Minds

Then Pharaoh said to Joseph, "Since God has revealed the meaning of the dreams to you, clearly no one else is as intelligent or wise as you are. You will be in charge of my court, and all my people will take orders from you. Only I, sitting on my throne, will have a rank higher than yours."

GENESIS 41:39–40 NLT

℘

Pharaoh called on Joseph to interpret his disturbing dreams, and the Hebrew came back with an even more disturbing answer: years of plenty were ahead, but so were years of famine. Joseph advised the ruler to put someone in charge of gathering the crops in the good years so they could be saved for the lean times to come.

Understanding that God had given Joseph this wisdom, Pharaoh and his advisers immediately agreed he was the man for the job. Though these men served pagan deities, their choice was no doubt directed by God. Without knowing it, they had made the wisest choice for the good of God's people, as well as their own.

Sometimes God steps in and changes the hearts of leaders, benefiting His own people. Or perhaps He changes the hearts of ordinary individuals, causing them to help Christians.

Has the heart and mind of an unbeliever been moved to help you? Have you thanked the Lord who caused that change? Remember, God doesn't only change the hearts of His own people; He rules the entire world.

Working for Good

*Someone who had escaped from the battle told Abram that
his nephew Lot had been taken away. Three hundred eighteen
of Abram's servants were fighting men, so he took them
and followed the enemy as far north as the city of Dan.*

GENESIS 14:13–14 CEV

Word came to Abram that a coalition army had captured his
nephew Lot.

As family members came, Lot probably wasn't on the top of
Abram's "most-loved" list. Given the opportunity to choose land for
himself, Lot took all the best, leaving the lesser land for his uncle
Abram. Who could blame an uncle for not having a lot of warm
feelings for such greed?

But Lot was still his nephew, and the younger man was in
serious trouble. So Abram honorably took all his troops and went
to his rescue. Perhaps Abram had recognized that he should have
given Lot a few limitations in his choice, or maybe, having seen the
sinfulness of Sodom, Abram was glad not to have to deal with that
territory. Whatever his thoughts, they didn't stop him from leading
his fighting men far north to Lot's rescue. And Abram was successful.

We've all had irritating relatives. Maybe they haven't been greedy,
like Lot, but they've done us wrong or made life difficult. Can we
take Abram for our example and choose to do good to the people
who have hurt us? Will we actively work to bless them, no matter
what they've done?

No Good Option

"Go and tell David, 'This is what the LORD says: I am giving you three options. Choose one of them for me to carry out against you.'"
1 CHRONICLES 21:10 NIV

In taking a census of Israel, David sinned. First Chronicles 21:1 specifically tells us the act was incited by Satan. Even Commander Joab's objection to it hadn't stopped the king, so he had no one else to blame for his wrongdoing.

God decided to punish Israel and, through the seer Gad, placed this choice before the king: three years of famine; three months of warfare, in which Israel would lose to her enemies; or three days of a God-sent plague.

David grieved over the instantaneous choice he had to make. Finally, he told Gad he'd rather be in God's hands than his enemies'. The Lord sent a plague that took the lives of seventy thousand men, but as His angel was about to touch Jerusalem, He relented. Repentant David asked that punishment should not affect the innocent people of his city but offered up his own family instead.

Sometimes, especially when we've fallen into sin, our own options don't look very good. Will we suffer for a long time with continual and painful damage, be attacked by our enemies, or have a brief but painful time under God's hand? The choice is best left in the hand of our Lord God. Whether we've fallen into sin or stayed faithful, He can still head us in the right direction.

Pillar of Salt?

But [Lot's] wife looked back from behind him,
and she became a pillar of salt.

GENESIS 19:26 KJV

un for your lives! And don't look back or stop anywhere in the valley! Escape to the mountains, or you will be swept away!" an angel warned Lot and his family as he pushed them toward safety (v. 17 NLT).

But not everyone in the family was anxious to leave Sodom. Lot's unnamed wife couldn't go without a last look at her home. Perhaps it held too many fond memories or some secret sin enticed her. Something drew her eyes in the wrong direction, and for her disobedience, she became a salt pillar.

Lot's wife isn't the only one who looks back longingly on the past. We may look back to pasts that held good things, but not the best ones God had for us. As the angels pull us in a more difficult direction, we too can long for the easy road of sin.

We may not become pillars of salt, if we turn to linger in our pasts or dwell on painful memories that have never quite lost their grip on our lives. But we're also unlikely to make the most of our todays when we're constantly looking over our shoulders. If bitterness for past wrongs fills our hearts, it keeps us from focusing on the forgiveness and joy God has for us today.

Make the right choice, and let the past be the past. God has a wonderful present for you now. Embrace it thoroughly.

Moral Ground of Goodness

*"When you go through deep waters, I will be with you.
When you go through rivers of difficulty, you will not drown.
When you walk through the fire of oppression, you will not
be burned up; the flames will not consume you."*

ISAIAH 43:2 NLT

Have you ever made a biblical decision you foresaw would bring flak from others? While you knew you had no other option, looking down the road, you knew others would make you sorry for that choice. And that's just what happened. Maybe you lost a job because of it or bore the brunt of extended criticism—or had a thousand other things make your life miserable.

Making right choices, biblical ones, is not always going to be popular. No matter how much they claim to be open-minded, those who defy God don't always allow Christians to peacefully coexist with them. And even some other believers can object to a biblical decision.

Should we roll over for every person who disagrees with us? Are we so tuned in to niceness that we lose track of the moral ground of goodness that the Lord wants us to stand on?

God doesn't promise that we will be free of critics. He doesn't say our lives will always be smooth. But He does say He will walk with us the whole way. He will protect us from destruction.

Do we have courage to do right and stand firm on Him?

Humble Pie?

Peter spoke up, "Even if all the others reject you, I never will!"
Jesus replied, "This very night before a rooster crows twice,
you will say three times that you don't know me."
MARK 14:29–30 CEV

Peter knew he would never make the kind of bad decision that would separate him from the Lord. Deny Jesus? It was unthinkable! Peter was one of the three men who were closest to the Master. Jesus' aims were Peter's aims, and the disciple thought he'd rather die than forsake Him. So when Jesus started warning His disciples they would fall away, the fisherman immediately stood up and corrected Him.

Proud Peter couldn't imagine he'd do such a thing once, much less three times. But when the situation got dangerous, his courage fled and he found himself doing that unthinkable thing. Just as Jesus predicted, faithful Peter did worse than any of the others and denied his Lord three times.

All of us, especially those of us with a history of good decisions, need to beware of pride. We may be tempted to criticize those who have made bad choices. But we need to realize that in the right situation, all of us can respond in a foolish way. If Peter could fail, so can we.

Just as his rejections of the Master came as a surprise to Peter, our own failures may surprise us. But by remaining humble when we make good choices, we may eat less humble pie later.

Do You Love Me?

The third time he said to him, "Simon son of John, do you love me?" Peter was hurt because Jesus asked him the third time, "Do you love me?" He said, "Lord, you know all things; you know that I love you." Jesus said, "Feed my sheep."

JOHN 21:17 NIV

The pain of denying his Lord struck Peter's heart deeply. The Gospel of Mark, based on his testimony, doesn't even include this story of Jesus' forgiveness and the restitution of Peter's place among the apostles, though Mark certainly must have known the story. Peter's close friend John tenderly tells us of these events that all the apostles must have viewed.

What freedom his Lord's forgiveness brought Peter, but it came to a new person. The Peter we see after the Resurrection is a chastened man who is deeply aware of his own ability to fail. Putting brazenness behind him, Peter becomes the kind of leader God needed for His fledgling church—a church that told the story of the death of the beloved Savior and His resurrection. The new Peter combined deep faith with self-control. By then, both the new church and the stronger apostle were aware that faith did not only encompass joy but also pain and failure.

All of us, even those of us who love our Lord deeply, have it in us to fail gloriously. But, like Peter, through our failures, God may bring us to new understandings of Himself, ourselves, and our ministry to others. Then our Lord will call us to return. Do we love Him enough to choose to follow that call?

Bad Plan

Lot was afraid to stay on in Zoar. So he took his two daughters and moved to a cave in the hill country. One day his older daughter said to her sister, "Our father is old, and there are no men anywhere for us to marry. Let's get our father drunk! Then we can sleep with him and have children."

GENESIS 19:30–32 CEV

*W*hat were Lot's daughters thinking? How did the older one come up with this plan? Perhaps her troubles destroyed her ability to think clearly, because taking this action cut her off from respectable society. Certainly no man in her day and age would have wanted to marry a woman who had slept with her father—and what if she had not conceived, or had a girl? Where would she have been then?

Sometimes we are amazed at the ability of people to think so wrongly. But this unnamed woman gives us an idea of how that happens. Separated from all she knew, having endured a terrible disaster in her life, she reached out for any straw of hope. A son to protect her, she thought. That would solve her problems.

Had she considered the difficulties of raising a child alone? The many years before he'd be able to protect her? The attitude of others when they discovered who his father was? The anger of her own father? Her flimsy straw of hope wouldn't help much. Couldn't she simply have put her trust in God, knowing He would provide a husband?

Our plans or God's—which will we choose?

Problem or Blame?

〜〜〜〜〜〜〜〜〜〜〜

*Then Sarai said to Abram, "You are responsible for
the wrong I am suffering. I put my slave in your arms,
and now that she knows she is pregnant, she despises
me. May the LORD judge between you and me."*

GENESIS 16:5 NIV

Sarai made a decision, and it didn't turn out well. To have a
child to fulfill God's promise, she made her own plan and
gave her maid, Hagar, to her husband. The idea was that the slave
would bear a child who would belong to Sarai.

Sarai didn't imagine that the maid would have a will of her
own and treat her disrespectfully. In their small camp of people, the
tension must have been nearly unbearable.

Sarai "solved" the problem by conveniently forgetting her own
choice and blaming her husband—a common solution for many
unhappy wives. Stuck in a vise, with no good way out, Abram told his
wife to do as she pleased. That didn't end in a happy situation either,
but it kept Abram from experiencing his wife's sharp displeasure
in the short term.

Blaming others for our own poor decisions doesn't solve anything,
does it? Sarai didn't end up with a happy family life, and neither
do we.

It's better to fix the problem than the blame. Taking credit for
our own mistakes may not solve everything, but at least it will allow
people to admire our character and will not make them angry at
us for unfair criticism.

What are we fixing today?

Keep It Honest

Jacob said to Laban, "The time is up, and I want to marry Rachel now!" So Laban gave a big feast and invited all their neighbors. But that evening he brought Leah to Jacob, who married her and spent the night with her.

GENESIS 29:21–23 CEV

ommunication is a big part of decision-making, whether it relates to understanding the details of a problem or interacting with another person. But some forms of communication can stop understanding in its tracks. Lying is one of them.

Jacob came to Laban and clearly expressed his desire to marry Rachel, the daughter he'd worked seven years for.

Without comment, Laban set out all the wedding trimmings, invited the neighbors, and brought a woman to Jacob's tent that night. After celebrating heartily, the groom consummated the marriage, only to discover in the morning that he had the wrong bride.

Then communication got really heated!

When we want to have good decisions and good relationships, lying is not on our agenda. For many reasons God tells us to be truthful, but, practically speaking, a lack of truth always has the potential to cause trouble, just as it did here. The two men's relationship goes downhill from this point on.

It's the same for our relationships. When we decide to tell the truth and deal with problems up front, we may have to battle through some conflict, but we don't immediately lose our reputations and add the flames of resentment to the situation.

Whatever we do in our decision-making, we need to remain honest.

Other Ideas

[Laban said,] "Wait until the bridal week is over; then we'll give you Rachel, too—provided you promise to work another seven years for me." So Jacob agreed to work seven more years. A week after Jacob had married Leah, Laban gave him Rachel, too. . . . So Jacob slept with Rachel, too, and he loved her much more than Leah. He then stayed and worked for Laban the additional seven years.

GENESIS 29:27–28, 30 NLT

As decision-making skills go, this wasn't one of Jacob's best moments. Perhaps if he'd been able to see what this choice would bring to his future, he might have reconsidered. Having two wives, sisters who competed for his affections, didn't create a pretty family life.

Still, it was a hard choice, losing the woman he loved because of his father-in-law's dishonesty; and in some cultures, having more than one wife was acceptable. It wasn't as if Jacob was without examples that seemed to condone his action.

God made it clear that marriage was to be one man, one woman from the very first, but some men refused to follow that. Their results haven't been happier than Jacob's—and certainly not for the women and children.

Today, other cultures and religions have ideas that go against Christian, biblical instruction. Are we to follow them? If we do, we may find ourselves in a similar situation to Jacob's, whose unharmonious family relations are something we'd never want to repeat.

The Best Plan

*So they nominated two men: Joseph called Barsabbas
(also known as Justus) and Matthias. Then they prayed,
"Lord, you know everyone's heart. Show us which of these
two you have chosen to take over this apostolic ministry,
which Judas left to go where he belongs."*
ACTS 1:23–25 NIV

By nominating two men to take Judas's place, the disciples meant well. The work of the church needed to go on, and it seemed logical to get help for their mission. But they could hardly have been more wrong in making that choice themselves.

Scripture doesn't tell us if they prayed much before this, though it should have been a decision bathed in prayer. Instead, it seems as if they barged ahead, asked God's blessing on their own ideas and choices, and made something of a mess of things. God already had His eye on the right man for the job, but it was someone who hadn't even committed to Him yet—an enemy of all Christians.

The apostles could never have found the right man because they'd never have looked at Saul of Tarsus. And Saul wasn't ready for the job yet.

We never hear anything more of Matthias. Though he may have been an upstanding, devoted Christian, he wasn't the man God had in mind to use to reach the Gentiles. Saul had just the skill set God needed for that task.

Do we follow in the apostles' footsteps and run ahead of God in our decision-making? Or can we wait for a while, knowing He will soon reveal the best plan?

One Small Decision

One day Dinah, the daughter of Jacob and Leah, went to
visit some of the young women who lived in the area.
But when the local prince, Shechem son of Hamor the
Hivite, saw Dinah, he seized her and raped her.
GENESIS 34:1–2 NLT

No question about it, the bulk of the blame for Dinah's rape falls on Shechem and his unbridled passions. He looked, liked, and acted on impulse, with no thought for the consequences. Certainly he never cared what this would do to Dinah's life. He made an awful choice with terrible results for Dinah, himself, and his people.

But that awful decision would never have happened had Dinah also not made a bad decision. Here she was in a strange place, and she went out alone. You might compare it to a lone woman going out in a less-than-savory neighborhood today.

Though Dinah's mistake doesn't remove the blame that can be placed on Shechem, it did open her up to the rape. Savviness about dangers is something both genders need to have, but women just have to look out for themselves in ways that men don't. It's not fair, but it's the way things are.

One small decision had an impact on Dinah's life. It's the same with us. Are we careful about the places we go, always considering how they could affect us physically or morally? Do we use good judgment about the people we spend a lot of time with? Those small choices can impact our lives, though perhaps differently from Dinah's.

Wise Advice

*The way of fools seems right to them,
but the wise listen to advice.*
PROVERBS 12:15 NIV

ride in our own decision-making skills might be a warning sign, because it's easy to think we've made great choices, but seeing our weaknesses is another matter. We all like to feel good about our own abilities, and we may get overly enthusiastic about them.

Humility isn't a popular attitude because it's a hard one, but it's still wise. And wise people seek out advice, especially when they know they're not very knowledgeable in a subject.

If you aren't a carpenter and you need to make a bookcase, it would be wise to talk to your neighbor who spends his days working with wood. No one will look down on you for seeking advice from an expert. But so often people want to rush ahead under their own power, and they end up with lengths of wood that are too short and nails that just aren't up to the job.

How are our spiritual lives different from such a household project? If anything, spiritual advice is more important. What we do with our worldly lives only affects us for a few years, but spiritual choices can last eternally.

Let's be sure, though, that we are getting wise advice. Does our adviser suggest ways that agree with the Word? Is her theology consistent and careful, or is she involved in a group that's doubtful? We need to choose advisers wisely and follow them only as far as they follow God's Word.

A World of Difference

*They said to you, "In the last times there will be scoffers who will
follow their own ungodly desires." These are the people who divide you,
who follow mere natural instincts and do not have the Spirit. But
you, dear friends, by building yourselves up in your most holy faith
and praying in the Holy Spirit, keep yourselves in God's love.*

JUDE 1:18–21 NIV

Ungodly people can be found anywhere, sometimes even in
the last place you'd expect them—within the church. But no
church is free of those who are struggling in their faith or people
who are seeking but have yet to be found by the Lord. Perhaps that's
why some church divisions take place so easily.

The New Testament church struggled with men such as Simon,
who wanted to buy the power of the Holy Spirit (Acts 8:18–19). And
the Corinthian church was nearly torn apart by those who easily
fell into sin. Whether it's one of the original churches planted by
Paul and his men or a church today, division is one of the powerful
tools Satan uses to separate God's people from Him and each other.

Under such circumstances, decision-making becomes especially
challenging for church leaders and members. But Jude gives us
God's advice to the faithful: build yourselves up in faith and pray,
keeping yourselves in God's love.

Love, not ungodliness, makes a world of difference.

Time to Trust

*Peace I leave with you, my peace I give unto you:
not as the world giveth, give I unto you. Let not your
heart be troubled, neither let it be afraid.*

JOHN 14:27 KJV

Decision-making has its scary days. Large, life-changing choices often make us feel as if we're poking into a dark cave. We can't see into the future to know for certain that this is the best for us, our families, and our communities.

How do we know we are on the right track? Often we simply feel a sense of God's peace. We've prayed, counseled with others, thought of all the issues that might face us. We've done our best and can only rest in the hope that this is the place God wants us to be in right now. So we move forward in faith, asking God to show us if we're headed in the wrong direction.

God's peace can be a hard-won thing. It may not come overnight, and as we seek the peace that passes all understanding, we may have sleepless nights, wondering if we've made a mistake. All the while, we have prayed, asking God to show us the right direction.

Now is the time to trust God, knowing that He communicates with us and wants us to make wise choices. Simply putting our futures in His hands and trusting that He will lead us in the right way is worth more than all the worrying we could do.

Free Choice

*Christ has set us free! This means we are really free. Now hold on to
your freedom and don't ever become slaves of the Law again.*
GALATIANS 5:1 CEV

One of the biggest decisions the leaders of the New Testament
church had to make was whether or not they would require
the Gentiles to be circumcised. Circumcision was a sign of the Jews'
covenant with God—by it, men indicated their connection with
the faith.

Jesus never addressed the issue of circumcision. After all, His
disciples had gone through the rite when they were infants. It would
only be an issue of the early church once many Greeks became part
of the church. Who could blame the new converts for hesitating to
undergo such pain unless it was strictly necessary?

But there was more than physical pain to this question. The
church leaders needed to address theological issues: Would requiring
circumcision lead the church back to obeying the Law? How did
this relate to believers' freedom in Christ? The Jerusalem Council,
after much debate and seeking the input of the apostle Paul, chose
not to require the rite.

Not every decision is a landmark one like this one. The council
no doubt made many ordinary choices that never got recorded. But
when they had to step out and call a shot that wouldn't be popular
with their own people, they didn't back down.

We don't have to back down either when we make a choice that
glorifies Him. Freedom in Christ is freedom to do right.

Admire People, Obey God

It is the LORD your God you must follow, and him you must revere. Keep his commands and obey him; serve him and hold fast to him.

DEUTERONOMY 13:4 NIV

It's good to have people, especially good decision-makers, to follow. Seeing those who make good choices in action helps us find our own way in discovering good options for our lives. But let's recognize that people can only take us so far. Every human being is flawed, so none of us make perfect choices. We may write books on how to make wise decisions, show the way in our work or personal lives, and encourage others to do well, but none of us should have blind followers.

God is the One whom we each need to put first in our lives. While we can admire humans, we are not called upon to revere them. They are not God, and their limitations show up quickly. They cannot see the flaws in us and in others that will affect our lives seriously. God alone can give us the best guidelines, through His Word. When another person gives advice that runs counter to scripture, we know which way we need to go.

Admire people, learn from them, but single-mindedly follow the Lord. Don't let others distract you from the good God wants in your life. Serve Him, hold fast to Him, and your decisions are much more likely to be successful.

Decision-Making Picture

〜〜〜

*Sir, we will do just what you have said. Our wives and children and
sheep and cattle will stay here in the towns in Gilead. But those of us
who are prepared for battle will cross the Jordan and fight for the* LORD.

NUMBERS 32:25–27 CEV

〜

The tribes of Reuben and Gad came to Jazer and Gilead, east of
the Jordan River, and saw land perfectly suited to their cattle
and sheep. So they went to Moses and asked if they could settle there.

Moses didn't have a problem with their taking the land, but he
worried that this choice would mean that Israel would go into the
Promised Land without two tribes' worth of warriors. Letting two
tribes go could mean the others would balk at going into God's
Promised Land too. Soon, none of them would be obeying the Lord.

So Reuben and Gad proposed that the two tribes leave their
flocks and families behind and the warriors would head west with
the rest of the tribes. They would fight God's battle, then return to
their property.

Moses carefully stated the terms of their agreement, and the tribes'
representatives repeated it back to him. Both sides understood what
was expected. Then Reuben and Gad fulfilled the promise to their
fellow Jews.

God gives us a beautiful example of group decision-making in
these verses. Both sides discussed, considered the problems, and
came to a compromise. Both followed through on their part of the
agreement.

That's a good picture of decision-making today too. Can it become
part of our practices?

Turned Around

*And I am convinced that nothing can ever separate us from
God's love. Neither death nor life, neither angels nor demons,
neither our fears for today nor our worries about tomorrow—
not even the powers of hell can separate us from God's love.*

ROMANS 8:38 NLT

Nothing, not even wrong decisions, can separate us from God.
That's not to say that if we did something sinful we can
avoid confessing it—we do, and we need to turn from that sin. But
no bad choice is unforgivable, and most can be turned around. God
doesn't hold a wrong choice against us and shun us. Instead, He
wants us to bring that situation to Him in prayer, ask forgiveness for
any wrongdoing, and seek His help for a new plan. There's always
a second chance for those who love Jesus.

When we make a terrible choice, or even a bundle of them, we
need not be stuck forever. Though we may have to painfully rework
our bad choices and make changes over time, God never withholds
His love from us. He supports us as we faithfully seek to rebuild our
lives.

As we redesign things, seek others' forgiveness, and otherwise
clean things up, we can be certain God will help us in our rebuilding
project. That's the business He's in, after all.

Have a plan that's gone amiss? Don't be afraid to turn to the One
who loves you best. If angels, demons, and fears can't separate you
from Him, a bad choice never will.

Wild Hopes

[Moses' mother] became pregnant and gave birth to a son. When she saw that he was a fine child, she hid him for three months. But when she could hide him no longer, she got a papyrus basket for him and coated it with tar and pitch. Then she placed the child in it and put it among the reeds along the bank of the Nile.

EXODUS 2:2–3 NIV

What a nerve-racking decision this was for Moses' mother. Since Pharaoh had declared that all male Israelites should be killed, she knew she could not keep her son. If anyone discovered the boy, his life would be over.

So in a wild hope that her son would be saved, she set him adrift on the Nile River in a pitch-covered basket, with only his young sister to watch over him.

Most of us know the rest of the story. The baby was saved by Pharaoh's daughter and went on to become the Old Testament's most important prophet.

Moses' mother did so many things right in her decision-making: She thought outside the box and protected her child, even in the basket. But most of all, she based her actions on God's will. There was no doubt in her mind that this life was precious and worth saving. No act of Pharaoh could change that, and she depended on God to protect her family and save her child.

When we make choices, will we follow God's law, despite the risks? Will we stand up for the right, when danger seems to lurk all around? Then our wild hopes may not be so wild.

Keeping an Oath

The men of Gibeon quickly sent messengers to Joshua at his camp in Gilgal. "Don't abandon your servants now!" they pleaded. "Come at once! Save us! Help us! For all the Amorite kings who live in the hill country have joined forces to attack us." So Joshua and his entire army, including his best warriors, left Gilgal and set out for Gibeon.

JOSHUA 10:6–7 NLT

The Gibeonites had pulled a fast one on the Jews. They pretended to be distant neighbors and sought a peace treaty with Israel. Once Joshua gave them one, he discovered these people lived in his backyard, northwest of the city that would become Jerusalem.

Having given an oath, the Israelites were bound by it. But imagine the chutzpah of the Gibeonites when the Amorites attacked them and they expected Israel to come to their aid.

Joshua probably pondered this decision. Should he hold to the promise or be glad to see someone else wipe out people who could be a danger to the Jews? Was it wise to go to their aid, putting his soldiers at risk?

But Joshua knew how seriously God took an oath: "A man who makes a vow to the LORD or makes a pledge under oath must never break it. He must do exactly what he said he would do" (Numbers 30:2 NLT). So he went ahead and defended the liars. God brought Israel victory.

When we promise to do something, will we also choose to follow through? God will be faithful when we are.

Ask, Seek, Knock

"Ask and it will be given to you; seek and you will find;
knock and the door will be opened to you."

MATTHEW 7:7 NIV

Nineteenth-century evangelist George Mueller built five orphanages, at a cost of one hundred thousand pounds, yet he decided early on never to ask anyone for help funding his ministry. Nor did Mueller go into debt to keep his work going. He prayed, trusting that God would provide, and He always did.

One day, having been told that there was no food for them, Mueller had the children sit in their places and thank God for their meal. As they were waiting, the local baker came with loaves of bread for them; he had just known that Mueller would need the bread and brought him three batches that he had made that night. Then the milkman's cart broke down, and he completed the meal with his donation of milk that would otherwise have spoiled.

During Mueller's life, his orphanages housed over ten thousand children who went into trades, domestic service, or were trained for a profession. Reportedly, the local mines and factories had a hard time finding unskilled young workers because of Mueller's work to educate and find places for the orphans. Throughout his life, he founded one hundred and seventeen schools that educated over a hundred and twenty thousand students.

Are you in need? You need only choose to share that need with God and consistently trust in Him. Ask, seek, knock, and He will open a door, just in time.

Kinder, Gentler Choices

To some who were confident of their own righteousness and looked down on everyone else, Jesus told this parable: "Two men went up to the temple to pray, one a Pharisee and the other a tax collector."
LUKE 18:9–10 NIV

Anyone who has read the Gospels can tell you that Jesus and the Pharisees had many differences. This group of strictly religious men saw themselves as keepers of the faith, and they didn't approve of Jesus and His teachings. At many points in His ministry, Jesus had to interact with these self-righteous folks.

Sometimes Jesus chose to challenge the Pharisees head-on; at other times, as in this instance, He got His point across more gently. Seeing their self-righteous attitudes, He didn't beat them up with their own wrongdoing. Instead, He used a gentler approach that could indirectly reach their hearts. Jesus told a story with the point He wanted to make clear.

Sometimes, whether it's to a child or a coworker, we have to get a point across that might not go down so well. Confrontation is unlikely to do more than create ill feeling, but we know we need to address the issue. Like Jesus, when we face confrontation, we can defuse things by deciding not to hit someone in the face with our point—we can tell a story that gets the idea across without criticism or ask questions instead of whaling in with a solution.

A choice like that could be a turning point in the lives of everyone present.

The Best Answer

*If any of you need wisdom, you should ask God,
and it will be given to you. God is generous
and won't correct you for asking.*

JAMES 1:5 CEV

Ask financial advice of a person who knows a lot about money, and you probably won't get much for free. She can't afford to give away knowledge and wisdom that cost her much trouble to learn. Everyone needs to make a living, so that's only fair. Though people can be generous, they all have many needs that interfere with their ability to help anyone freely. And even people who know much have limits; some decisions seem to defy human help.

Maybe we've talked to the people who know, and they seem unable to adequately advise us. Perhaps they tell us we really need to pray about the situation. That may seem like a frustrating excuse, but it's not bad advice.

No matter how much or how little humans help us with our decisions, we have another, more powerful resource who has all the wisdom we need, no matter what choice we face. God isn't a heavenly Father who limits our prayer time or the amount of advice He'll give. He won't tell us we're wrong to ask again. Instead, we'll get the full benefit of His wisdom, no matter what we're asking for and how much we are in need. And it's all for free.

Need a solution to a thorny problem? Whether it's a spiritual conundrum or a decision between two good options, turn to God. He'll always help you find the best answer.

Faith Is the Difference

*But when you ask for something, you must have faith
and not doubt. Anyone who doubts is like an
ocean wave tossed around in a storm.*

JAMES 1:6 CEV

Have you turned to God for help and, instead of finding Him just over your shoulder, He seemed to have disappeared? *What's going on here?* you may have wondered. *Didn't He say He'd always be with me? Where did He go? How can I choose an alternative without Him?*

Maybe God didn't change—you did. Instead of trusting in the truths He's shown you, you began to let doubt slide a filthy pane of glass between you and your Lord. He's there, but you just can't see Him because so much unbelief has gotten between you.

When we seek God's wisdom, we need to trust that He will provide it and that what He provides will lead us in the right direction. There's no point in asking for advice we plan to doubt. Acting like that with your best friend might cause her to withdraw too. And how much greater is this wisdom God wants to share?

"Now faith is confidence in what we hope for and assurance about what we do not see" Hebrews 11:1 (NIV) tells us. If we can see the end of our decision, it is not faith. The trusting one stands firm in God's promises, no matter what she sees.

Are you standing firm or tossing on the ocean? Faith is the difference.

The Choice in Our Hands

I pray that your love will keep on growing and that you will
fully know and understand how to make the right choices.
Then you will still be pure and innocent when Christ returns.
And until that day, Jesus Christ will keep you busy doing
good deeds that bring glory and praise to God.
PHILIPPIANS 1:9–11 CEV

Paul's prayer for the Philippian church was that it would continue to grow, even when he was not there to lead it. He'd appointed church leaders, filled them with as much teaching as possible, and given them into the charge of the Holy Spirit. Now the choices were up to the church and its leaders. Paul had placed the ability to make good, biblical decisions in their hands; the Holy Spirit had filled them, making them able to follow God's will. The Philippians had everything they needed. But Paul was still concerned.

Sometimes we need to train another in Christ's ways and leave the decisions in her hands. We've done our best in giving her the good information she needs. Now her decisions are a matter of her own judgment and faith.

We can put the tools of decision-making in another person's hands, but we cannot make the choices for her any more than God makes all our choices for us. Eventually, we give her freedom to make mistakes—and learn from them.

At that point, we understand how God feels when He lets us choose. Will we follow Him or another? Will we obey? The choice is in our hands.

Living Right

Throughout the night, my heart searches for you, because your decisions show everyone on this earth how to live right.

*G*od's judgment is beyond anything we could imagine in our own lives. With it, He rules our world, the galaxies beyond ours, and all of His massive creation. His wisdom made everything that exists, from the tiniest bug to the largest planet. And all He has made works together with absolute perfection when it's under His control. Only when things fall into sinful humanity's hands do they start to fall apart.

God chooses perfectly, no matter if He's making that bug or establishing the laws by which His children should live. So when He calls us to right living, or righteousness, it's because He knows what works best. After all, He made people, their world, and the situations they find themselves in.

Living by God's rules is right living, because these laws cause us not to sin, and provide a happy, healthful life and the means to make the most of our days. When we live according to the Creator's plan, we avoid many toxic things, both physically and emotionally. Life runs more smoothly in the Lord's hands than when we're solely in control.

Depending on God's judgment instead of our own brings us into harmony with Him and with our world. Whether we need advice in the middle of the night or at high noon, our Lord is always available and always right.

Who would want to live any other way?

Any-Hour Guidance

I praise you, LORD, for being my guide. Even in the darkest night, your teachings fill my mind. I will always look to you, as you stand beside me and protect me from fear. With all my heart, I will celebrate, and I can safely rest.

PSALM 16:7–9 CEV

No matter what the hour, God's guidance is always available for our lives. If we land in a hospital at two in the morning or simply lie awake with a thorny problem, we are not alone—we always have our Lord to connect with. Peace can be ours when we seek His advice and comfort through the Word.

The need for guidance doesn't always come at convenient times, and anguish faces us at odd moments. Or perhaps, at an even more convenient moment, we simply don't know whom to turn to.

We know that giving in to the agony of worry is pointless. How could we change anything with anxiety? But where do we go when the questions remain unanswered and the pain overwhelms us? God's Word has an answer for us. Though the Lord may not give us a complete answer in the middle of the night, He can bring us faith and comfort and sleep that will prepare us for the decisions that are part of a new day. And when that day comes, He offers strength for our needs.

When the choices are hard, safely rest in God. Lean on Him for strength, and you will have all you need.

Songs of Praise

You give me strength and guide me right. You make my feet run
as fast as those of a deer, and you help me stand on the mountains.
PSALM 18:32–33 CEV

David had made many instantaneous decisions. After he became a courtier to King Saul and risked his life in battle for him, the king took a dislike to the man who now led his armies. One day, David ran from Saul and was let down out of his window by his wife, Saul's daughter, who wanted to save his life. With the help of Saul's son and David's best friend, Jonathan, David escaped.

From then on, David always seemed to be just a step ahead of his enemy. When he spoke about running, David spoke from experience, for Saul's soldiers chased him about the land until he had to ally himself with pagan kings to avoid conflict with Israel. The entire time, this savvy battle commander had to make swift decisions on how to best obey God and not harm the king while still defending his own life.

Finally David experienced victory and wrote Psalm 18, praising the Lord who had protected him, made his choices good ones, and scattered his enemies.

If our choices seem more like battle plans than decisions, David has advice for us. Like him, we can lean on our Protector and Savior, and someday we too may soon sing songs of praise.

Band-Aid Solutions

But Hamor said to them, "My son Shechem has his heart set on
your daughter. Please give her to him as his wife. Intermarry with us;
give us your daughters and take our daughters for yourselves."
GENESIS 34:8–10 NIV

As women, we cringe at Hamor's words. His son had raped Dinah. How could this man see that as an act of love? Dinah, we probably think, would be better off without Shechem.

Even if she had married him, what of their uneven outlook on faith? That was likely to create another big problem!

It doesn't take us long to discover that those who do not share our faith come to different decisions, often ones that just seem incomprehensible to those of us who follow the Bible. Morality influences choices, and obviously Hamor's morals were weak. Perhaps he was looking for a quick, easy solution to a political problem and misrepresented his son's feelings. Fearful that the Hebrews would respond to violence with violence, he looked for a Band-Aid to slap onto the problem.

But Band-Aids, unless they cover small cuts, don't work very well. They aren't made to solve serious relationship problems, and Hamor's solution was destined to fail—Dinah's brothers weren't about to accept it.

Are we too trying to solve our big problems with quick fixes that really don't fix anything? Like Hamor, we are unlikely to see a happy ending. Instead, let's dig deeper for a permanent solution—one that reflects God's will.

Yoked to Sin?

So Moses said to Israel's judges, "Each of you must put to death those of your people who have yoked themselves to the Baal of Peor." Then an Israelite man brought into the camp a Midianite woman right before the eyes of Moses and the whole assembly of Israel while they were weeping at the entrance to the tent of meeting.

NUMBERS 25:5–6 NIV

J ust as Moses commanded Israel's judges to put to death those who had fallen into sin with pagan women and worshipped their gods, as if it were stage managed, an Israelite walked into the camp with a Midianite woman. No sooner were God's words of judgment out of Moses' mouth than the two entered the man's tent. So flagrant was their sin, they made no effort to hide it, nor did there seem to be any expectation that others would object. After all, this man wasn't the only one who went to their neighbors' dwellings with that purpose in mind. But how many foolishly walked into the camp with these women?

He and the woman became an object lesson for all Israel, as Aaron's grandson, Phineas, destroyed the two sinners with a single spear. Their deaths ended the plague that had fallen upon the nation because of the sin they personified.

Like Israel, we are prone to sin. Will our deviations from God's path be brief and quickly rectified, or like this unnamed man, will we be so yoked to sin that we put our lives and spirits at risk?

Winking at sin could be more dangerous than we expect.

Desert Living?

~~~

Caleb tried to quiet the people as they stood before Moses. "Let's go at once to take the land," he said. "We can certainly conquer it!" But the other men who had explored the land with him disagreed. "We can't go up against them! They are stronger than we are!"

NUMBERS 13:30–31 NLT

Vibrant Caleb encouraged the Israelites to enter the Promised Land. "We can do it!" he told the doubters among them. Joshua agreed. Both men saw the good things in the land and the power of God that had led the people so far. What nation could beat God?

But the other ten men who explored the land could only see the power of the enemy. Their strength looked overwhelming. So ten explorers nixed the idea of taking the land God had offered to His people.

Had this nation of former slaves gone to the new land in their own strength, there's no doubt that Caleb and Joshua would have been eternal optimists. Even such a large nation as theirs would have had a hard battle against so many enemies, considering their lack of fighting experience and weaponry. But God's people had a secret weapon more powerful than any battle equipment the enemy could bring to bear: God Himself went with them. And He provided the battle plans.

The nation went with the majority opinion and ended up spending forty years in a desert.

When God shows us His plan, will we step up and own it? Or will we decide to spend forty years in a desert of our own making?

In Good Company

Jesus sent out the twelve apostles with these instructions. . . .
As you go, announce that the kingdom of heaven will soon be here.
Heal the sick, raise the dead to life, heal people who have leprosy, and
force out demons. You received without paying, now give without being
paid. Don't take along any gold, silver, or copper coins. And don't carry
a traveling bag or an extra shirt or sandals or a walking stick.
MATTHEW 10:5, 7–10 CEV

tepping out on their new mission, the disciples had to be both excited and nervous. Theirs was a large ministry, and one that would receive both criticism and praise. They'd face many hard situations.

The Twelve went out in the clothes they stood in, nothing extra. Like the lilies of the field, they depended on God's care for everything. Though they could heal the sick, raise the dead, and cast out demons, Jesus specifically forbade them from taking any means of support with them.

With such abilities, perhaps God knew the Twelve could become overly proud of the gifts He had given, so He made them entirely rely on Him for their daily bread, clean clothes, and shelter. As they traveled, they would constantly need these things.

When the challenges we face seem to hang us in midair, we are in good company. If God provided for His disciples, can He not care for us too? Will we choose to rely on Him?

Glorifying Someone

Then they said, "Come, let us build ourselves a city,
with a tower that reaches to the heavens, so that we may
make a name for ourselves; otherwise we will be
scattered over the face of the whole earth."
GENESIS 11:4 NIV

It didn't take all that long after Noah and his family survived the flood for humankind to fall into sin again. The message of salvation that should have gripped hearts was so much less appealing than human self-confidence and wrongdoing. As today, sin seemed so much more attractive than godliness.

But a desire to connect with something larger than man remained in those postdiluvian human hearts. Warped by sin, it caused these people to build a tower stretching heavenward. The worship the builders most desired was of their own skills at construction, not God.

Though God had commanded humanity to fill His earth and multiply (Genesis 9:1), these proud people planned to remain in a single place, focused in one large city. The outcome of their plan was never in doubt. Before they had time to bind themselves together in sin, God changed their ways of speech. No longer sharing the same language, they could not communicate, and work stopped on the city that had become a testament to man's pride.

Are we building a testament to our own pride? We must recognize it and choose another direction. All we build glorifies someone—will it be God or ourselves?

Criticism or Commitment?

As Pharaoh approached, the people of Israel looked up and panicked when they saw the Egyptians overtaking them. They cried out to the LORD, and they said to Moses, "Why did you bring us out here to die in the wilderness? Weren't there enough graves for us in Egypt? What have you done to us? Why did you make us leave Egypt?"

EXODUS 14:10–11 NLT

You'd think one way to avoid criticism would be to follow God very closely indeed, wouldn't you?

Well, you'd be wrong.

The same folks who criticize God for not removing all pain and suffering from this world are constantly on faithful ones' cases about one thing or another that displeases them.

Moses was up to his chin in gripes. As he and the Israelites stood with their backs to the Red Sea, the people started a complaintfest. Before giving God a chance to rescue them, they criticized His prophet. And that wouldn't be the last time the great prophet got a tongue-lashing from his people.

Of course, God came through and saved the Israelites in a stunning fashion that even nonbelievers know about (they've all seen Charlton Heston leading God's people through the dry path between two walls of sea). Yet it didn't stop the complaints.

Deciding to follow God has nothing to do with the objections of others. It's our decision, and one we need to cling to, no matter how many people open their mouths to complain. Faithfulness isn't about popularity but commitment.

So when critics multiply, check your status with God and stand firm. Then you'll know you're headed in the right direction.

Dead from Embarrassment?

Then the two from Emmaus told their story of how Jesus
had appeared to them as they were walking along the road,
and how they had recognized him as he was breaking the bread.
LUKE 24:35 NLT

Sharing the story of how they met Jesus and didn't even recognize Him didn't show the two Christians on the road to Emmaus in their finest light. Discouraged at the death of their Savior, the two had begun the seven-mile journey from Jerusalem. Along the way, they met a man who seemed not to know the story of Jesus' death. Eagerly, they told the tale.

"You foolish people! You find it so hard to believe all that the prophets wrote in the Scriptures. Wasn't it clearly predicted that the Messiah would have to suffer all these things before entering his glory?" the stranger replied (Luke 24:25–26 NLT). Then He explained the scriptures to them. As they sat down to a meal with Him, suddenly their eyes were opened, and they knew Jesus.

Though they may have looked a bit foolish, the two returned to Jerusalem and faithfully told their story to the Eleven, sharing the Resurrection message.

In our lives too, there will be times when we must choose between looking foolish and doing the right thing, whether it's for God's kingdom or the world. Let's remember that no one has ever died of embarrassment from choosing the right way.

Like Caleb?

"Now give me this hill country that the LORD promised me that day. You yourself heard then that the Anakites were there and their cities were large and fortified, but, the LORD helping me, I will drive them out just as he said."
JOSHUA 14:12 NIV

Eighty-five-year-old Caleb had lost none of his determination. When he'd returned from scouting the Promised Land forty-five years before, Moses promised the hill country to him for faithful service to the nation. Now, in a time of life when most people would have been seeking out a rocking chair, Caleb was preparing to take to the battlefield. And he'd be facing the very people who had caused the fearful ten spies to advise Israel to turn back from the mission God had directed them to fulfill.

Forty-five years before, Caleb had believed God could bring His people successfully into the Promised Land, and his faith had not changed, though his body might have become frailer. Scripture tells of the success of Caleb's attack in a general account of the conquest: "So Joshua took the entire land, just as the LORD had directed Moses, and he gave it as an inheritance to Israel according to their tribal divisions. Then the land had rest from war" (Joshua 11:23 NIV).

When God gives us a task, will we turn back for a time? That doesn't mean it will not be ours to fulfill in the future. But we too can waste years preparing for a task God would already have had us complete.

Will we be like Caleb or his fearful people?

Enough?

*David said to Saul, "Let no one lose heart on account of this
Philistine; your servant will go and fight him. . . . The L*ORD
*who rescued me from the paw of the lion and the paw of the
bear will rescue me from the hand of this Philistine."*
1 SAMUEL 17:32, 37 NIV

Young David came to the Israelite camp and saw strong men
quail before Philistine champion Goliath. All Israel's armor
and muscle seemed frail before the might of one nine-foot, nine-
inch-tall opponent.

When David looked at this man, did he suddenly shrink to a
more normal size? Did David's weapons become more powerful?
No. Goliath remained the same strong man. But David, unlike his
fellow Israelites, realized that he *was* a man—and as such, he had a
weak spot.

That flaw? Goliath did not have God on his side. His pagan gods
could never stand up for him. They had not parted the Red Sea
and brought a nation into a land filled with powerful enemies who
toppled before them.

Israel had a history with God and knew His power, but faced
with one nine-foot man, everyone—except David—forgot it all. This
young man avoided King Saul's protective gear and made a choice
to go into battle with a slingshot and five smooth stones.

With God aiming his weapon for him, that was enough.

Will God be enough for your fight? You too have a history with
Him and know His power. Is that enough?

Poor Choices

So Simeon and Levi, two of Dinah's brothers, attacked with their swords and killed every man in town, including Hamor and Shechem. Then they took Dinah and left. . . . Jacob said to Simeon and Levi, "Look what you've done! Now I'm in real trouble with the Canaanites and Perizzites who live around here. There aren't many of us, and if they attack, they'll kill everyone in my household."

GENESIS 34:25–26, 30 CEV

No man will treat our sister this way! Dinah's brothers determined. In retaliation for her rape, full brothers Simeon and Levi attacked and destroyed the people of Shechem.

Obviously, their father wouldn't have approved of their plan, so they did it on the sly. After their attack was completed, Jacob simply had to pick up the pieces. God told the family to move on to Bethel to avoid the fury of the surrounding nations.

Were Jacob's objections to his son's actions the opinion of God too? The Bible doesn't tell us. Was God in favor of reducing the threat of pagan influences on Israel? Would He have done it another way? We cannot know. The two siblings never gave God the chance to bring about His own justice.

God brought His people into safety again. He protected them, despite this murderous act. Scripture never tells us of any punishment meted out to these men—but it never tells of missed blessings either.

Sometimes God gets us out of hot water, even when we've not done His perfect will. But let's not mistake that for approval of our poor choices.

The Currency of Heaven

Then he said, "Beware! Guard against every kind of greed.
Life is not measured by how much you own."
LUKE 12:15 NLT

Money and possessions appear as if they'll add so much to our lives. We think they provide long-term security, so we put effort into gaining more of them.

As we add to our possessions, we eventually discover that things only give a very temporary joy. However much we love the things of this world, after a while, they become mundane. We start living as if they were simply our due, and they become background to our ever-increasing desires for more stuff.

But when emotional or spiritual trouble comes our way, we quickly begin to understand that all the stuff in the world can't bring permanent happiness. We could own everything in this world and not have love, peace, and joy in our lives. Trite but true: money can't buy happiness.

Happy people sometimes live very frugally. Unhappy ones sometimes have all the toys the world offers.

Thankfully, God doesn't measure anyone by her possessions— He is only interested in her heart. A heart filled with greed has no room for love, and as God's Word says: "If I gave everything I have to the poor and even sacrificed my body, I could boast about it; but if I didn't love others, I would have gained nothing" (1 Corinthians 13:3 NLT).

The currency of heaven is not money, stocks, or bonds but love. Without it, happiness cannot be ours. Choose love, and joy will fill the corners of your life mere things can never pervade.

Tipping the Scale

Unfailing love and faithfulness make atonement for sin.
By fearing the LORD, *people avoid evil.*
PROVERBS 16:6 NLT

To be Christians, we don't need some hidden spiritual knowledge; loving God is the simple basis for our faith, the bedrock of our relationship with Him. Though our love and faithfulness cannot earn salvation, they show our appreciation for all He has given. God's unfailing love and faithfulness have made the atonement. But as we live for Him, sin becomes less and less part of our lives, and we show forth His grace.

Daily choices lie before us: how we treat others when life is difficult; the words we say when we speak to friends, family, and perfect strangers; the time we spend with God or in other pursuits. We constantly, and sometimes unconsciously, make decisions that show the value we place on spirituality and our Lord.

At the base of every choice is our attitude concerning God and evil. Non-Christians may deny their existence, or they may have another view of the "balance" between good and evil, but scripture is clear: our choices weigh in on the side of love and faithfulness to God or the evil that draws us from Him.

Will our scales tip on the godly side or swing downward into sin? Let us tip our lives toward God in every choice and begin to exemplify the love that bought us out of sin. On less-than-perfect days, let's come to Him for forgiveness and again weight the scale in His direction.

Wonderful Surprise

So then, those who suffer according to God's will should commit themselves to their faithful Creator and continue to do good.

1 PETER 4:19 NIV

Choices don't always come in pretty packages. Sometimes suffering becomes an unavoidable part of our decisions, and we may be tempted to choose an unwise path of least resistance that just leads to more pain.

Suffering doesn't mean we've necessarily made a terrible choice in the past (though that is possible). We may have fallen into a trap caused by another person's mistake or sin. Or, though we have turned from sin, it may still be working its way out of our lives as we work out our salvation.

However the pain has come, be encouraged that God has not deserted you. As Timothy Keller says, "God is accomplishing [the defeat of evil] not in spite of suffering, agony, and loss but *through* it." If we are part of His mission of salvation, suffering will affect us and influence our decision-making. But it need not cause a disaster.

Suffering must not derail our good choices. As we commit ourselves to our Lord, continuing to obey His Word and making the decisions commanded there, God's work in our lives becomes a clear testimony. And through our godly actions, we touch others who need His mercy and grace.

Pain is never a good excuse for wrongdoing because sin only compromises our choices and leads to increased suffering.

Let's cling to our Lord through the hurts, and the package we open in the end will be His wonderful surprise.

Faithful to Whom?

But Doeg the Edomite, who was standing with Saul's officials, said, "I saw the son of Jesse come to Ahimelek son of Ahitub at Nob. Ahimelek inquired of the LORD for him; he also gave him provisions and the sword of Goliath the Philistine."

1 SAMUEL 22:9–10 NIV

On the run from his angry master, David came to the priest Ahimelek for help. The kindly priest chose to give King Saul's servant help. But Ahimelek didn't know a spy would carry news of his simple deeds back to the king.

The innocent priest knew David's character and had little worry about handing him a sword with which David claimed he'd serve his king. Ahimelek did it because he knew his man. Confronted by Saul, he replied: "Who of all your servants is as loyal as David, the king's son-in-law, captain of your bodyguard and highly respected in your household?" (v. 14 NIV). Ahimelek was no traitor, just God's faithful man who stood his ground. But his choice cost him his life, since the demented king saw nothing but danger.

Doeg, the second decision-maker in this story, simply comes across as a spy and tattletale. While we admire Ahimelek, Doeg the spy leaves a sour taste in our mouths. We can hardly believe God would let him live and take the life of the faithful man.

Faithfulness may have a price. Will we, like Ahimelek, deserve a good reputation, follow God, and pay that price? Or will we lose all honor, like Doeg?

Ripple Decisions

*"I will make your descendants as numerous as the stars
in the sky and will give them all these lands, and through
your offspring all nations on earth will be blessed, because
Abraham obeyed me and did everything I required of him,
keeping my commands, my decrees and my instructions."*
GENESIS 26:4–5 NIV

Faced with a famine, Isaac had to decide what to do. Should he move his family to more-prosperous Egypt or stay on in the land God promised to His people? As their survival teetered on a knife's edge, Isaac needed to make one of the most important decisions of his life.

That's when God came to him and spoke these words. After telling Isaac to stay in the land, He renewed the promise He'd made to his father. Because of Abraham's choice and the God-instituted covenant between them, the Almighty would bless all Abraham's offspring.

Abraham had set a blessed course for his family by choosing obedience to the Lord. One man's choice to obey God affected a whole people. But his son's follow-up decision was just as important. Isaac could have derailed Israel's future instead of confirming it.

When God calls us to make life choices, do we ponder the impact that could have on our futures and the lives of others? Like the ripple a stone thrown into water causes, the consequences of some choices spread out across our lives. Will we make decisions in obedience to God's will for our destinies, bathing them in prayer? He is the only One who can see where those ripples will end. Why would we fail to seek His wisdom?

Choose to Share It

The LORD said to Moses and Aaron, "Get away from all these people so that I may instantly destroy them!" But Moses and Aaron fell face down on the ground. "O God," they pleaded, "you are the God who gives breath to all creatures. Must you be angry with all the people when only one man sins?" And the LORD said to Moses, "Then tell all the people to get away from the tents of Korah, Dathan, and Abiram."

NUMBERS 16:20–24 NLT

Angry at Korah's rebellion that led others astray, God was ready to destroy His people.

Moses and Aaron probably weren't too happy with their people at that point either, but they knew God's mercy and immediately asked Him to provide it for the innocent ones who stood near the sinners. God relented, and all those who stood aside from the ringleaders, their families, and their possessions were saved. But the earth swallowed up the wicked men, their households, and their followers.

That event must have been the topic of discussion for a long time in the remaining tents. By example, it was a powerful testimony to both grace and judgment.

When we read this story, do we feel like the Israelites, mercifully saved from disaster? Or are we like Moses and his brother, who desperately worked to save others from sin? Either way, we need to be aware of God's mercy in our lives and the lives of others (irritating as they may be) and choose to share those truths.

A Trusting Choice

*But I trust in your unfailing love. I will rejoice because you
have rescued me. I will sing to the LORD because he is good to me.*
PSALM 13:5–6 NLT

When life seems very dark, we may need to resolve to trust in
God. Though He has not shown the solution to our problem,
it doesn't mean one is not on the way. Rescue, after all, is God's
business. Just as the psalmist knew without a doubt that God would
come to his aid, we can be certain He is waiting to help us too.

First, let's look to our past. How many past good things have we
already received from our Lord? Will we look to them and know that
His blessings have not ended in our lives? Or will we allow doubt
to fill our minds and hearts?

Though God's rescue may not look just as we expect, we can
be certain it will come. He brought us into His kingdom and has
promised never to leave or forsake us (Hebrews 13:5). Even sparrows,
small, insignificant birds, are known by the Father and do not fall
without His knowledge. How much more will He care for our needs
(Matthew 10:29–31)?

Trusting God is not a one-time choice, though that is how our
relationship begins. The decision to trust lies before us every day,
through many circumstances. As we rely on Him, repeatedly and
patiently, we experience His good works.

Will we trust Him today?

A Nervous Choice

All the people took the gold rings from their ears and brought them to Aaron. Then Aaron took the gold, melted it down, and molded it into the shape of a calf. When the people saw it, they exclaimed, "O Israel, these are the gods who brought you out of the land of Egypt!"

Exodus 32:3–4 NLT

While Moses tarried on Mount Sinai, his people became very nervous. Had the prophet deserted them? Even worse, had God?

A majority of the Hebrews must have believed that, since they came to Aaron and asked for a new set of gods—not just one—to take His place. Maybe they figured that having more than one would be safer?

Aaron unwisely gave in to community pressure. Asking them to donate their gold to the project, he melted it down and created a golden calf. Bulls were common deities in the Middle East.

It's possible that in some confused way, Aaron was trying to lead the people back to God, because in the next verse he declares: "Tomorrow will be a festival to the Lord!" (NLT). He used the term *Yahweh*, a name not applied to pagan gods. But if he had good motives, the priest's plan went far awry. Neither God nor the people got that message (see v. 8).

Standing up for God is a critical choice for every Christian. The persecuted church has stood firm, denying those who call on them to worship other gods. May we join them by taking a firm stand for our Lord, no matter how nervous we feel.

Clear Choices

Come close to God, and God will come close to you.
Wash your hands, you sinners; purify your hearts,
for your loyalty is divided between God and the world.
JAMES 4:8 NLT

Feeling double-minded about a decision? *Should I go this way? Or that? What if. . . ? Will God approve if I make this choice?*

Scripture has advice for that situation. It's very simple: Draw close to God and begin to feel His presence. Cleanse your actions and heart, putting sin at a distance. Then you're ready to obey Him.

We question our decisions when we have no clear vision for the future. The way looks hard or some worldly temptation plunges us into doubt. Perhaps the push and pull of the spirit and the world create doubt in our hearts.

At such a moment, we need to hold off on serious decision-making and simply follow God one step at a time. We may need to seek God's face until sin loses its power and He clarifies the direction He has for our lives.

Focusing on the Lord and simply obeying the part of His will He has already revealed to us can relieve our doubts. If prayer is all we can do, let us pray faithfully and frequently. We need to trust that He will make a way for us and make it clear in His own time.

As we wait, what once seemed doubtful and dark may suddenly become clear as God opens doors in answer to our prayer. When that happens, we can walk through them with confidence.

A Faith-Filled Decision

*But the officer said, "Lord, I'm not good enough for you to come
into my house. Just give the order, and my servant will get well.
I have officers who give orders to me, and I have soldiers who
take orders from me. I can say to one of them, 'Go!' and he goes.
I can say to another, 'Come!' and he comes. I can say to
my servant, 'Do this!' and he will do it."*

MATTHEW 8:8–9 CEV

How important that sick servant must have been to the centurion, since he was willing to humble himself before Jesus to ask for the man's healing. This officer of Rome was part of the nation that dominated Israel, and many Jews undoubtedly resented him. Requesting a Jewish healer's aid would have been unusual indeed.

The centurion was aware of that—and of the fact that Jesus' entry in his home would cause Him to be defiled, so he didn't insist on Jesus coming there. Knowing of the power of the Lord, he applied a truth from his own life and trusted Jesus enough to believe that whatever He said would come to pass.

When we turn to God in our decision-making, can we trust as this centurion did? We don't have to have some special pull with God if we are simply His children. He loves us and wants to answer. Will we trust that He will respond to our needs and prayers?

Eyes on Jesus

*Peter replied, "Lord, if it is really you, tell me to come to
you on the water." "Come on!" Jesus said. Peter then got out
of the boat and started walking on the water toward him.
But when Peter saw how strong the wind was, he was
afraid and started sinking. "Save me, Lord!" he shouted.*
MATTHEW 14:28–30 CEV

agerly, Peter asked Jesus to let him walk on water, and the
Master encouraged him to step out of the boat. But as the disciple began his unusual walk, the strong wind dragged his eyes off the Savior.

Suddenly Peter's ankles became wet, then his legs. Did he have water up to his knees? The vigorous disciple knew where to go for help. Calling on Jesus to save him, he felt the grasp of the carpenter's strong hand. "You of little faith," He said, "why did you doubt?" (v. 31 NIV).

Has God called you to walk on water? Perhaps you've become involved in a challenging ministry, and the way has not been easy. Or maybe your job is overly challenging. Did God call you to this service? Then do not doubt. Move forward into the water, trusting that His hand will bear you up. Do not let any human hand break your grasp on the Master's. Though distractions and unreasonable critics may come your way, they are not from God. Do not let them end the work He has set before you.

Once you have put your hand to the plow, cut a straight furrow. You'll only do that when your eyes are on Jesus.

Hand Washing

When Pilate saw that he was getting nowhere, but that instead an uproar was starting, he took water and washed his hands in front of the crowd. "I am innocent of this man's blood," he said. "It is your responsibility!"

MATTHEW 27:24 NIV

Pilate faced a tough decision. He knew what was right, but he also knew that if he didn't cave in to the Jewish leaders' demands to kill Jesus, he could have a riot—or worse—on his hands. Rome didn't leave governors with such troubles in power very long, and Pilate wanted to keep his lucrative job. So he went against all that he knew was right and condemned an innocent man.

Certainly Pilate knew it wasn't a great decision because he washed his hands of the impossible situation and blamed the Jewish leaders, avoiding responsibility for his actions. But there was a problem in that: None of us can avoid responsibility for our decisions. Washing hands may be symbolic, but it does not erase sin that causes a poor choice. Though God certainly knew the blame that belonged to the Jews, a bowl of water and a towel could not exonerate Pilate.

Are we tempted to throw the blame elsewhere and cheaply exonerate ourselves? Just as it did not work for Pilate, it won't work for us. If we're standing there with wet hands, let's turn to the only One who can truly make us clean.

Scot-free

To the Jews who had believed him, Jesus said, "If you hold to my teaching, you are really my disciples. Then you will know the truth, and the truth will set you free." They answered him, "We are Abraham's descendants and have never been slaves of anyone. How can you say that we shall be set free?"

JOHN 8:31–33 NIV

What do You mean? these new believers wondered. Hadn't they been brought up in God's truth for their whole lives? Was Jesus accusing them of being slaves to a foreign nation? Immediately, they got offended.

But Jesus wasn't talking about Rome, which ground its heel into Israel, or even Egypt, where their forefathers had been slaves for four hundred years. He meant something much more personal. Their personal "relationship" with sin held them in bondage.

These new believers reacted out of their old life beliefs, expecting the Judaism they'd been brought up in to be their salvation. But Jesus had something much more freeing to offer if they'd put their spiritual lives in His hands. First they had to make a choice between belief systems.

In our spiritual lives, we too have decisions to make. Will our former lives hold us in bondage, or will we trust in the freedom of the Savior? At times His forgiveness may seem free to the point of looseness: Why should someone who harmed us be forgiven and get off scot-free? But the forgiveness freedom God gives to us He offers to others too, and so must we.

Will we give as freely as we've received?

A Barn-Load of Blessings

Then [the rich fool] said, "This is what I'll do. I will tear down my barns and build bigger ones, and there I will store my surplus grain. And I'll say to myself, 'You have plenty of grain laid up for many years. Take life easy; eat, drink and be merry.'"

LUKE 12:18–19 NIV

The rich fool planned on being the ultimate party guy. All the money he gained from his business success would fund his stomach and his pleasures. Life, he expected, would be one entertaining day after another. No cares should get in the way of enjoyment, and his large store of goods would fund his new lifestyle.

The future looked good, until God devastated him by demanding his life of him that night.

God called this man a fool because instead of putting his money into things that served a good and godly purpose, he wasted it on purely selfish and worldly expenses. Had he generously given to God and His people, his story might have been very different, but the man had had no time for God.

When we need to make giving decisions, let's keep the rich fool in mind. Being stingy with our money may hoard up a few more dollars, but it will not gain us the blessings only God can give.

If we want a barn-load of blessings, let's look to our Lord, not our own gain. He will never fail to reward us in unimaginable ways.

An Attitude of Ingratitude

*But the people [of Israel] grew impatient with the long journey,
and they began to speak against God and Moses. "Why have
you brought us out of Egypt to die here in the wilderness?" they
complained. "There is nothing to eat here and nothing to drink.
And we hate this horrible manna!" So the LORD sent poisonous
snakes among the people, and many were bitten and died.*
NUMBERS 21:4–6 NLT

On their trip to the Promised Land, the Israelites wearied of their travel. Perfect travel arrangements didn't exist back then—they walked the whole way. As they wearily trudged along, they began to complain. God's provision of monotonous manna for food didn't please them, so they compared their current lot to their place in Egypt. Suddenly well-fed slavery didn't look so bad.

Conveniently, when their tastebuds became tempted, they forgot the worst of their former life. The pain of slavery, beatings, and misuse by their masters faded as the trials of the Exodus increased.

God does not tolerate whining and complaining very well. When He's given His people so much, ingratitude is not an option. So He sent snakes out among the people, and many confirmed whiners died. Still, all they had to do to avoid death was turn to the bronze snake God had Moses put on a pole. As they turned to Him, their sins were forgiven, and they lived.

We too have the option to complain or seek the Savior. Will we appreciate all God has done or develop an attitude of ingratitude?

Chief Decision-Maker

A man was there by the name of Zacchaeus; he was a chief tax
collector and was wealthy. He wanted to see who Jesus was,
but because he was short he could not see over the crowd.
So he ran ahead and climbed a sycamore-fig tree
to see him, since Jesus was coming that way.
LUKE 19:2–4 NIV

*C*urious Zacchaeus unknowingly made a really good decision, even though he might have felt rather silly climbing a tree at his age. This tax collector wasn't a faithful Jew. He simply wanted to see the man who performed miracles—yet he ended up in a life-changing meeting with Jesus.

Sometimes, like Zacchaeus, our everyday desires unexpectedly propel us into the right place. As with this small man, God uses ordinary events to draw us to Himself. He reaches out to us, and we need only respond with a yes.

Despite all our careful decision-making, some things simply lie in God's hands. When He wants to create change in our lives, He may simply bring it to us, whether we are on the ground at the front of the crowd or hanging out in a tree, desperate for something new. When God places that new thing in our hands, it's up to us to reach out thankfully and accept His invitation.

All the careful, well-thought-out decisions we make only get us so far. No matter how good or bad our choices, we need to recognize that ultimately, God directs our lives. Sometimes He steps in unexpectedly; other times He responds to our faithful walk with Him. Either way, He is still our chief decision-maker.

You Might Also Like . . .

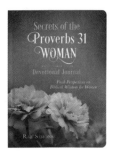

Secrets of the Proverbs 31 Woman Devotional Journal

This lovely devotional journal, offering equal parts inspiration and encouragement, will uncover the "secrets" of the Proverbs 31 woman. Each reading, tied to a theme from Proverbs 31:10–31, is rooted in biblical truth and spiritual wisdom. Women of all ages will be inspired to emulate the virtues extolled in this memorable passage of scripture.
Hardback / 978-1-68322-554-6 / $19.99

The Mother's Secret of a Happy Life
Daily Devotional Journal

The Mother's Secret of a Happy Life Daily Devotional Journal—based on the beloved classic *The Christian's Secret of a Happy Life* by Hannah Whitall Smith—promises practical, personal, and powerful encouragement for moms of all ages. This timely take on a favored classic offers inspiration for moms seeking a life overflowing with joy and purpose—life at its absolute best!
Hardback / 978-1-68322-418-1 / $19.99